NEW YORK CENTRAL
R A I L R O A D

Brian Solomon with Mike Schafer

MBI Publishing Company

First published in 1999 by MBI Publishing Company, 729 Prospect Avenue, PO Box 1, Osceola, WI 54020-0001 USA

The information in this book is true and complete to the best of our knowledge. All recommendations are made without any guarantee on the part of the author or Publisher, who also disclaim any liability incurred in connection with the use of this data or specific details.

We recognize that some words, model names and designations, for example, mentioned herein are the property of the trademark holder. We use them for identification purposes only. This is not an official publication.

MBI Publishing Company books are also available at discounts in bulk quantity for industrial or sales-promotional use. For details write to Special Sales Manager at Motorbooks International Wholesalers & Distributors, 729 Prospect Avenue, PO Box 1, Osceola, WI 54020-0001 USA.

Library of Congress Cataloging-in-Publication Data Available

ISBN 0-7603-0613-3

On the front cover: Though the New York Central had been gone for decades when this photo was taken in 1989, the railroad's spirit survived in a number of ways at the number of places. Here, one of Central New York Chapter–National Railway Historical Society's restored Electro-Motive E8-series passenger diesels gives spectators a glimpse of what it was like when the diesels were new early in the 1950s. *Jim Boyd.*

On the frontispiece: New York Central emblem on an Electro-Motive E-series passenger diesel on display at Essex, Connecticut. *Brian Solomon*

On the title page: Cruising along the Hudson River so closely associated with the New York Central Railroad—the "Water Level Route"—two passenger trains pass on a late summer afternoon in 1963 near Cold Spring, New York. At left, the Mohawk from Chicago is on the last leg of its journey to New York City; at right, the Ohio State Limited out of Grand Central is only about an hour into its overnight trip to Cincinnati. *Richard J. Solomon*

On the back cover: Clad in New York Central System's celebrated "lightning stripe" diesel-era paint scheme, a set of Electro-Motive F-series diesels idle away the late-night hours at the railroad's Detroit, Michigan, locomotive-servicing facility.

It's the summer of 1963, and the locomotives are likely facing a freight assignment southward to the Central's "Water Level Route" main line at Toledo, thence east to Cleveland, Ohio. *Hank Goerke*

Printed in Hong Kong

CONTENTS

ACKNOWLEDGMENTS

There was more to the New York Central Railroad than track, locomotives, freight and passenger cars, and depot buildings. It takes people—lots of them—working together to run a railroad, as illustrated by this Al Schultze photo of the Cold Springs, Ohio, tower operator handing up orders to the engineer of a freight headed by NYC Mikado No. 1984 on a summer day in the 1950s. Likewise, it takes the works of several to produce a book, even a modest endeavor such as this.

Research and fact verification (the latter an especially interesting task, since sources of early NYC history sometimes offer conflicting information!) is perhaps the most-time-consuming aspect of doing a history-related book, so first off the authors wish to thank C. W. "Chuck" Newton, a long-time devotee of the New York Central System. Charlie patiently answered our questions, reviewed our material, and pointed us in the right direction for both factual and photo sources.

In fact, photo acquisition just may be the trickiest part of putting together a history for a long-defunct railroad, and although we initially encountered some dead ends, eventually several folks came forth with some mighty interesting illustrative material. In particular we would like to thank Herbert H. Harwood Jr., Tim Doherty, Dave Oroszi, Alvin Schultze, Lou Marre, Bill Caloroso/Cal's Classics, Robert A. Buck, Paul Carver, Richard J. Solomon, J. R. Quinn, John Dziobko, Michael Sullivan, Ed Crist, C. W. Newton, Joe Welsh, Jay Williams/ Big Four Graphics, and the folks at Andover Junction Publications, the producer of this book, for access to the AJP illustration archives.

At the production end of this project, the authors give a tip of the hat to Maureene D. Gulbrandsen and Jim Popson, both of whom went beyond the call of duty to assist with design and production. And, a thank-you to the folks at MBI PublishingCompany, the publishers of *New York Central Color History,* for the final transformation into book form.

INTRODUCTION

Few American railroads are as steeped in lore and tradition as the New York Central System. To this once-great railroad that spanned the most populous quadrant of the United States, we can attribute several notable accomplishments: the invention of that all-American railroad icon, the caboose (on NYC predecessor Auburn & Syracuse in the 1840s); the launching of what is often considered the world's greatest passenger train, the *20th Century Limited* (1902-1967); the construction of one of the world's most renowned railroad depots, New York's Grand Central Terminal; the development of one of the all-time classic types of steam locomotive, the 4-6-4 Hudson (popularized by electric toy-train manufacturers American Flyer and Lionel); the pioneering of containerized freight transport, today a vanguard of modern railroading; and the creation of the famed New York–Chicago "Water Level Route" main line, a high-speed, nearly gradeless life line that to this day remains one of the most important freight and passenger transportation arteries in North America.

Whew! Those are mighty heady accomplishments for any company. They came at a price, however, and they did not happen overnight. But that's what this book is all about. *New York Central Color History* will provide insight as to how a rag tag collection of little independent railroads strung across Upstate New York early in the nineteenth century eventually metamorphosed into one of the all-time classic American railroads, one that served the nation's then-two-largest cities (New York and Chicago) as well as other commercial powerhouses—Cleveland, Boston, Detroit, St. Louis, Cincinnati, Indianapolis, Columbus, Toledo, Albany, and Pittsburgh.

But, reader beware. There is absolutely no way a comprehensive history of the NYC can be covered in 128 pages and some 120 photos. Rather, this book provides an historical overview and handy references (and certainly some degree of entertainment, especially when reading about the corporate shenanigans of railroading's notorious "Rail Baron" era in which NYC played a leading role through the indefatigable Vanderbilt dynasty) for basic matters relating to the armchair transportation historian. The text and illustrations have been chosen to provide readers with a feel for the life and times of the New York Central System and are not meant to document every aspect of the railroad's development and operations. There are numerous books, pamphlets, and magazine articles that have been published over the years that focus on specific NYC-related history and operations, and readers are encouraged to search out these items via the Internet or at various public train or railroadiana shows, railroad historical society meetings, or through ads in the various railroad-related periodicals.

And even for readers who are not old enough to have witnessed firsthand the New York Central, this book can prove a valuable perspective for observing and documenting today's railroading. Although the NYC has been gone for more than three decades, its legacy survives in many shapes and forms under the auspices of contemporary carriers, primarily Norfolk Southern and CSX Corporation through their recent bilateral acquisition of Conrail, but also Amtrak, Metro-North Commuter Railroad, Canadian National and Canadian Pacific, and numerous shortline railroads, among them the Finger Lakes Railroad, the Mohawk, Adirondack & Northern, the Adirondack Scenic Railroad, the Michigan Southern, and Ontario Midland.

Too, the Central spirit survives in hundreds of artifacts left behind by the railroad—several of which have been reproduced in this book—in the form of such collectibles as timetables, freight-schedule folders, passenger-train brochures, magazine ads, dining-car china, lanterns, switchlocks, and even commemorative plates such as that illustrated above (from 1956, illustrating the evolution of NYC locomotives). So, pull up an easy chair, flip to the following pages, and celebrate the life and times of one of America's greatest transportation companies, the New York Central System.

A map from a New York Central passenger timetable from 1954 shows the Central's system largely intact. Later in the 1950s, the railroad began some route rationalization that would render the West Shore segmented west of Albany and many of Michigan Central branches truncated. *Mike Schafer collection*

ART TO HEART!
and arrive at the
wn — close to hotels

4 TRAVEL AT *SEE* LEVEL!
Scenic close-ups of the Hudson and
Mohawk Rivers, Great Lakes, Berk-
shires.

5 RELAX ALL THE WAY!
No jitters when skies grow stormy.
No traffic strain when Central does
the driving.

6 ON THE LEVEL, YOU SLEEP . . .
along Central's gentle, *Water Level
Route* . . . traveling the safest way
on earth.

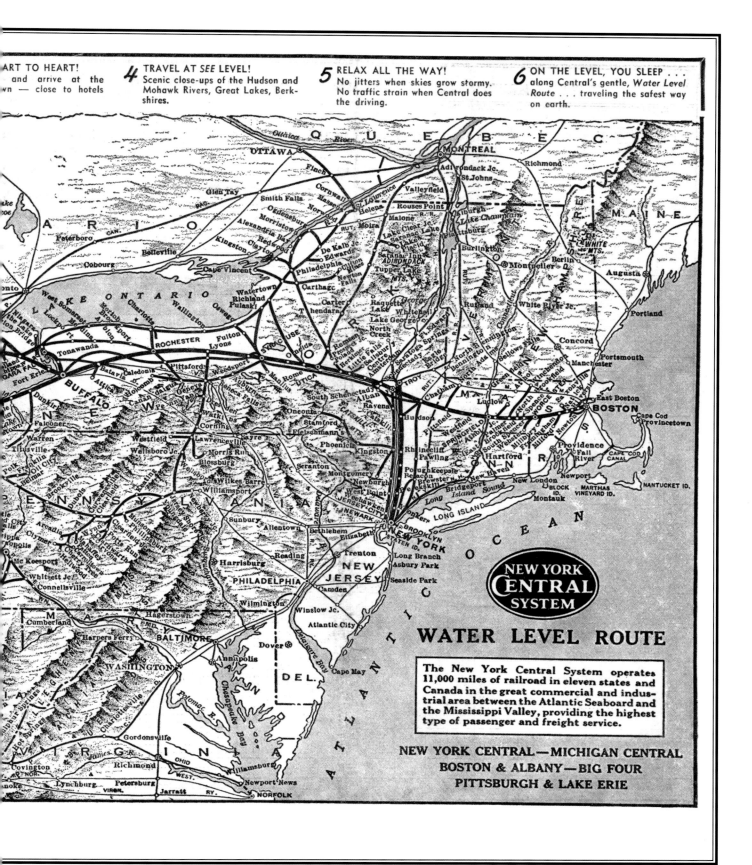

WATER LEVEL ROUTE

The New York Central System operates
11,000 miles of railroad in eleven states and
Canada in the great commercial and industrial area between the Atlantic Seaboard and
the Mississippi Valley, providing the highest
type of passenger and freight service.

**NEW YORK CENTRAL—MICHIGAN CENTRAL
BOSTON & ALBANY—BIG FOUR
PITTSBURGH & LAKE ERIE**

New York Central

The Scenic Water Level Route

Effective December 7, 1947
Form 1001

NEW YORK CENTRAL SYSTEM

The date is April 17, 1938. America is emerging from the worst depression in U.S. history; a Metro-Goldwyn-Mayer movie called *The Wizard of Oz* is in its final production stages; and over in Europe there are uneasy signs of strife. For the New York Central Railroad, however, it's business as usual as one of the road's Mohawk steam locomotives hustles along the Hudson River near Cold Spring, New York, with 142 freight cars that stretch all the way back to the Breakneck Ridge twin tunnels. It was a scene that was repeated several times a day on the "Water Level Route" during an era when the New York Central was a powerhouse in American transportation. In less than a decade, with World War II out of the way, NYC would present a new generation of railroad (LEFT) with diesel-powered trains. *Photo, H. W. Pontin, collection of Herbert H. Harwood Jr.; timetable, Mike Schafer collection*

DAWN OF THE NEW YORK CENTRAL

The *De Witt Clinton* Steams; Cornelius Vanderbilt Dreams

At its zenith, the New York Central was one of America's largest railroad systems. It operated more than 11,000 route-miles through eleven American states and two Canadian provinces. Hundreds of trains were scheduled every day, from branchline mixed freights and rural milk trains to named fast freights and the railroad's most famous passenger train: the glamorous, all-Pullman *20th Century Limited*.

Tens of thousands of people worked for the NYC, but no one individual could claim complete understanding of the Central's vast and complex operations. The railroad's four-track Water Level Route—one of the longest sections of four-track main line in the country—reached from New York City up the Hudson River to Albany, and then west across New York State to Buffalo. Although not entirely four tracks beyond Cleveland, Central's Lake Shore & Michigan Southern main line continued west to to Chicago by way of Toledo, Ohio, and South Bend, Indiana. Its Michigan Central lines reached from Buffalo to Detroit via Ontario and on to Chicago, with secondary lines to numerous points. The "Big Four Route"—the Cleveland, Cincinnati, Chicago & St. Louis—connected its namesake cities by way of Columbus, Ohio, and Indianapolis, Indiana, and operated numerous secondary lines throughout the Midwest. The railroad's Ohio Central lines reached across Ohio and into West Virginia coal country. Its Pittsburgh & Lake Erie affiliate connected the Pittsburgh region with the Central's trunk.

Central's Boston & Albany subsidiary crossed the Berkshires and reached to Boston, fulfilling the spirit of its name. The "West Shore"—so named because it closely followed the Hudson's west shore from Weehawken, New Jersey, to Albany—provided an alternative freight route to Buffalo. The Rome, Watertown & Ogdensburg, a network of secondary lines across northern Upstate New York, reached into Quebec.

New York Central's empire did not have one beginning, but many. Numerous small railroads were built that ultimately came under New York Central control. Each of its primary subsidiaries and affiliates has its own history that contributed to larger history of the NYC. Some of these companies were closely allied to NYC long before they were finally absorbed; others were not. New York Central System was never a truly single, unified railroad—although it certainly operated as such. Many of its larger subsidiaries retained considerable independence well into the twentieth century, and some affiliated lines, such Pittsburgh & Lake Erie, were never fully assimilated and actually separated from the company at the time of NYC's 1968 merger with the Pennsylvania Railroad.

MOHAWK & HUDSON

Not only was the Mohawk & Hudson the earliest New York Central predecessor, it was the first chartered railroad to be built in America. Its route along with a dozen others would come to form the basis for the *first* New

One by one, the windows close their eyes

... for a wonderful Water Level Route sleep

Nighttime on New York Central. Long ago, the last, leisurely dining car patron pushed back his chair with a contented sigh.

Only a few night owls still chat over refreshments in the club car. One by one, shades come down and lights go out as this great hotel-on-wheels glides along gentle, low-level valleys. The guests, in their Pullman private rooms, drift off to slumberland ... with a downy comfort and a deep-down sense of all-weather security no skyway or highway can match.

GOING OUR WAY? Throughout this area, you'll find New York Central streamliners and dreamliners to make your trips a daylight delight or an overnight vacation.

New York Central
The Water Level Route—You Can Sleep

The scenic Mohawk River in Upstate New York was a New York Central "neighbor" from the earliest days of the railroad. In this postwar magazine ad, the waterway provided an evocative setting for promoting nighttime travel on the NYC. *Mike Schafer collection*

York Central Railroad. The M&H was one of the first lines in North America to employ steam locomotives and "covered" freight cars—the boxcar.

The M&H was largely the vision of a George W. Featherstonhaugh, a wealthy cattle breeder of English descent living in the rural country west of Albany. He was among the world's earliest railway enthusiasts and paid close attention to railway developments in England. Primitive tram railways using horse-drawn wagons on wooden rails had a long history in England. After 1800, the development of the practical steam locomotive led to the first steam-powered train on those tram lines. In 1821, George Stephenson, one of the foremost railway engineers and locomotive designers of the day, chartered the Stockton & Darlington Railway in the north of England, a pioneering line generally heralded as the world's first steam-powered public railway. It finally opened for business in September 1825.

In the mid-1700s, England had begun building its inland canal system, which ultimately became one of the most highly developed canal networks in the world. Canals were considered a proven, efficient transportation system, and in the 1820s, New York State embarked upon building one the most ambitious canals in America. The famous Erie Canal connected Albany with Buffalo, thereby establishing an inland waterway across the interior of New York and linking the Great Lakes with the Hudson River. The Erie Canal opened for business only one month after the Stockton & Darlington.

A weak link in the Erie Canal was the particularly circuitous segment between Albany and Schenectady where the canal route wound around some 40 miles, compared to a mere 17 miles overland by road. The canal trip took a full day by boat, and stage operators were quick to take advantage of the canal's weakness, offering comparatively fast transport between these two cities. It was on this short route that George Featherstonhaugh envisioned building a railway. On December 28, 1825, a notice appeared in the *Schenectady Cabinet*:

> Application will be made to the legislature of the State of New-York, at the approaching session, for an act to incorporate the Mohawk and Hudson Rail Road Company, with an exclusive grant for a term of two years, for the construction of a Rail Road betwixt the Mohawk and Hudson rivers, with a capital of three hundred thousand dollars, if necessary; and to receive such certain tolls on the same, as may seem fit for the legislature to grant.—Dated December 19, 1825.

Frank W. Stevens, author of the book *The Beginnings of the New York Central Railroad*, attributes this anonymous notice to Featherstonhaugh. Initially there was opposition for the project from local stage companies, who rightfully viewed the railroad as a serious threat to their business, but Featherstonhaugh used his political influence to obtain a charter for his Mohawk & Hudson. During the railroad's formative years, Featherstonhaugh was closely involved with the railroad and traveled to England to inspect railway operations firsthand and meet with railway suppliers. However, before the first tracks were laid, Featherstonhaugh suffered a series of devastating personal losses. His two daughters died, followed by his wife, and later his house burned to the ground. He lost interest in the railroad, resigned, and moved to Philadelphia, letting others pick up where he left off.

John B. Jervis, a respected engineer who had worked on the Delaware & Hudson Canal Company where he experimented with railways, was hired to survey and build the line. Construction began in 1830 near Schenectady, and roughly a year later the Mohawk & Hudson was completed and ready for business.

The railroad inaugurated service August 9, 1831, using the *De Witt Clinton*, a locomotive built by the West Point Foundry in New York City. Great excitement accompanied the first excursions as thousands of people came out to witness the opening of the railroad. Trial runs proved challenging, as the M&H had little precedence on which to base its operations. No one on the railroad had ever run a train before, and just starting the locomotive was a new experience. When the engineer opened the little locomotive's throttle, the first train jerked violently, startling the passengers.

Compared to modern railroads, this was a primitive line, constructed using stone sleepers (ties) spaced three feet apart and wooden strap-iron rails. The railway was just under 16 miles long. Steep grades at both ends of the line in Albany and Schenectady required stationary steam engines to winch carriages up and down inclined planes into and out of the towns while regular locomotives moved the trains over the relatively level plateau between. The inclined planes remained in place for 13 years until a more suitable grade was constructed that permitted the use of adhesion locomotives over the entire length of the line.

Initially the railroad did not operate in the winter, apparently because of the railroad's reliance on the Erie Canal to forward traffic. The canal suspended operation when ice made passage impossible. Initially the M&H was strictly a passenger carrier, while freight traffic used the canal. In 1840, the railroad ordered 30 freight wagons and entered the freight business. Freight traffic was weak, and after a time the railroad discontinued through freight operations, though continuing to handle local business as needed.

THE UTICA & SCHENECTADY

The Mohawk & Hudson immediately inspired visions of a through railroad to Buffalo. In 1831 a proposal for such was put before the state legislature but was rejected. Fearful of railroad competition, canal interests did their best to keep railroads from being built. Gradually railroad proposals gained support, and during the 1830s a series of independent, short railways were chartered and constructed between Schenectady and Buffalo.

One of these was the Utica & Schenectady, a controversial line chartered on April 29, 1833. It was constructed 78 miles westward from Schenectady to Utica along the scenic Mohawk River, connecting such established

In a colorized scene dating from the early twentieth century, a trolley defers right of way to a New York Central passenger train invading the streets of downtown Syracuse, New York. When the Utica & Syracuse came to town in 1839, it did so literally, using Washington Street as its right-of-way. *Mike Schafer collection*

towns as Amsterdam, Canajoharie, and Herkimer through the natural cleft in the Appalachian range that the Erie Canal followed. Unlike the Mohawk & Hudson, which appeared to augment the Erie Canal, this line competed directly with the canal. Also, it was clearly a link in what might become an all-rail route between Albany and Buffalo. New York State had funded the Erie Canal, and it was not yet paid for. Strict regulations were passed that prohibited the U&S from hauling freight except for passenger's baggage. The line was completed in 1836, and when the first train arrived in Utica, the city's 10,000 residents celebrated wildly.

Although strictly a passenger carrier in its first eight years, the U&S enjoyed enormous success. Traffic grew briskly, and within a few years the line was converted to double-track operation. Erastus Corning, the railroad's first

president, was a successful businessman and a charismatic politician. He owned the prosperous Albany Iron Works, and during his career he variously served as Albany's mayor, a state senator, and as a Congressional representative.

THE SYRACUSE & UTICA

The next leg west was built by the Syracuse & Utica, a 53-mile line chartered on May 11, 1836, to connect its namesake cities. It opened for business in August 1839, and although it was required to pay heavy tolls to support the Erie Canal, it was permitted to move both freight and passengers. Most of its line passed through rural countryside and small towns, but to enter Syracuse the tracks rolled right down the city's main thoroughfare. Syracuse's Washington Street would gain notoriety as New York Central's primary mainline route for nearly a century. The sight of the *20th Century*

Limited rolling down the street behind a Hudson steam locomotive was a serious departure from one of Syracuse & Utica's diminutive locomotives hauling a few lightweight carriages down the same street.

WEST TO BUFFALO

Connecting with the Syracuse & Utica was the Auburn & Syracuse, chartered on May 1, 1834, and completed about the time of the S&U. The A&S did not directly parallel the canal and served Auburn, which the Erie Canal had bypassed. Initially the A&S was "horse-power" only, but after a short time locomotives took over. Eventually, the A&S would lay claim to being the birthplace of the caboose.

Another line, the Auburn & Rochester, continued 70 miles west to Rochester by way of Geneva, Manchester, and Canandaigua—three canal-less communities in need of improved transportation. Reaching west from Rochester, the Tonawanda Railroad predated most of its eastern connections. It was chartered on April 24, 1832—making it among the earliest railroads in the state—and built westward 34 miles to Batavia, reaching there in 1837. The first run to Batavia from Rochester was greeted by hundreds of exuberant Batavians who lined the tracks for a mile out of town in anticipation of the train. At that time, the railroad was an isolated operation primarily functioning as a feeder to the Erie Canal at Rochester. It remained isolated, even after the Auburn & Rochester line was completed into Rochester because the two railroads maintained separate terminals on opposite sides of town. Several years passed before they were finally connected. Rochester businessmen were in no hurry to bridge the gap between the two lines because stage operators, taxi drivers, and hotel and restaurant proprietors all profited from this disadvantage to travelers and shippers.

Although the Tonawanda envisioned completing a line all the way to Buffalo, serving communities south of the Erie Canal, its progress was stifled by the Panic of 1837, a financial crisis that slowed railroad progress all across the region. In 1842 it extended its line southward to Attica to connect with the Attica & Buffalo Railroad, which reached there at about the same time. Thus a little more than a decade after the opening of the Mohawk & Hudson, passengers were finally able to travel all the way from Albany to Buffalo by train. It would take a few more years before through service was offered, and shippers were still encouraged to use the Erie Canal. Other railroads were built to feed this Albany-Buffalo trunk: The Schenectady & Troy, for example, was a municipally owned railroad linking those two neighboring communities while the Rochester, Lockport & Niagara Falls was built to link those cities. Other lines were constructed to shorten the distance between the Hudson River and Lake Erie for through passengers, such as the Rochester & Syracuse, (formed from the merger of the Auburn & Syracuse and the Auburn & Rochester) which constructed a new direct route between its namesake points, leaving the original line via Auburn for local traffic. In 1850, the Buffalo & Rochester, formed by a merger between the Tonawanda Railroad and the Attica & Buffalo, built a new direct line west from

The much-sought-after destination of Buffalo was finally linked to Albany with an all-rail route in 1842. This post-card view of the NYC coach yards brimming with passenger equipment seems to indicate that a lot of folks were shuffling off to Buffalo as the new century got under way. *Mike Schafer collection*

Batavia to Buffalo while selling the Attica–Buffalo portion of the older route to New York & Lake Erie (later the Erie Railroad) interests.

PASSENGERS VERSUS FREIGHT

Today most American railroads are freight-haulers, and even during the glory years of the New York Central in the 1920s when the railroad was at the peak of its passenger business, the railroad generated the bulk of its revenue from freight. But in the formative years of New York State railroading, passengers were the primary emphasis, and for the first two decades passenger revenues were the railroad's primary concern.

Packet boats on the Erie Canal moved along at an average speed of just 4 mph, and while the ease of canal travel was a great improvement over early land travel, it could not compare to the relatively speedy transportation offered by the new railroads. Improved speeds were primarily seen as advantageous to passengers, but initially not viewed as necessary for freight traffic, especially when the additional cost of rail travel was considered. Furthermore, in the early years, legislation restricted some lines (the Utica & Schenectady being a prime example) from hauling through freight. Freight restrictions varied. Some lines were only penalized in the summer and autumn when the canal was open, but were allowed to move freight during the winter when the canal was closed. Tolls were imposed by the state on many lines to subsidize canal construction and operation. Railroads that connected with—but did not operate parallel to—the Erie Canal worked as canal feeders to communities that had been bypassed by the canal and typically were not subject to tolls. Freight traffic was considered a seasonal business, and most railroads in the region moved the majority of their freight traffic when the canal was out of service. The level of service was so affected that some lines stored their freight cars during the summer. The S&U had 1,800 feet of double-track sheds for storing its freight-car fleet. By 1850 the railroads had claimed nearly all passenger traffic, but the Erie Canal still carried the majority of freight.

Gradually, as the railroad network developed, the advantages of moving through freight became apparent. The railroads' economic and political power allowed them to make their case in the legislature and repeal freight-hauling prohibitions. By 1847 the restrictions on the Utica & Schenectady were lifted, and in December 1851 the railroads were freed from the burden of canal-supporting tolls. The results were quickly evident, and the amount freight traffic moving by rail between Buffalo and Albany grew dramatically in just a few years. According to Alvin Harlow in *The Road of the Century*, NYC component lines moved over 19.3 million ton-miles in 1851 and more than 51 million ton-miles in 1853. By 1856, the railroad was carrying more than 145 million ton-miles—more than a seven-fold increase in traffic. That year, revenue from freight operations surpassed passenger operations for the first time.

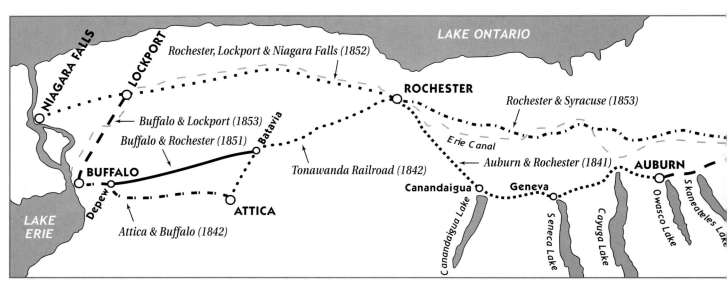

THE FIRST NEW YORK CENTRAL IS BORN

Consolidation of the various fledgling railway companies between Albany and Buffalo had numerous advantages. The railroads were already offering coordinated through service, and some smaller lines had already merged, but when a large-scale consolidation was discussed in 1847 and again in 1851, canal interests squelched the prospect of a single railroad across Upstate New York. Slowly, however, the railroads gained power and overcame the canal lobby. Finally, in 1853 the chain of Albany-to-Buffalo lines plus various branches and tributary lines were formally consolidated as the New York Central, a logical name for the new company which literally served the central portion of the state. At its birth, New York Central was among the most powerful financial entities in the U.S.

Erastus Corning, the successful leader of the Utica & Schenectady, led the new NYC. Once in command, he initiated systemwide improvements that included rail replacement and double tracking. The entire railroad between Albany and Buffalo featured two main tracks by 1860. These improvements were more than just beneficial to NYC—president Corning profited from this enterprise as much as the railroad, purchasing the majority of rail and iron products from his own Albany Iron Works. While he earned market value for his iron, he charged a nominal commission for each sale. He had been doing this for years with the U&S and did not see any wrongdoing

with this practice, which today would be viewed as a serious conflict of interest. Indeed, this practice soon warranted an investigation by company stockholders and others, and Corning was ultimately compelled to repay NYC a sum of roughly $10,000 representing his profits from iron sales to NYC. Despite this embarrassing episode, Corning remained in control of the Central for another decade, and under his leadership NYC set the groundwork for a through line to Chicago.

NEW YORK & HARLEM

The New York & Harlem was initially conceived as a horse-drawn passenger line, chartered in 1831 (the same year the Mohawk & Hudson inaugurated operations) to run on Manhattan Island from 23rd Street north to the Harlem River on the northern end of the island. In the 1830s, 23rd Street was considered "uptown," and the Harlem line was later extended a few blocks farther downtown to better serve its riders. Gradually the railroad built northward beyond Manhattan Island. It reached Fordham, in the Bronx, in 1841 and White Plains in 1844. In 1852 the NY&H reached its northern terminus at Chatham, New York, 129 miles out of Manhattan. At Chatham a connection was established with the Western Railroad (of Massachusetts), a future component of the Boston & Albany. The Harlem was among the nation's very earliest suburban lines—the Harlem offered regular passengers discounted rates to encourage frequent travel—and suburbs developed along

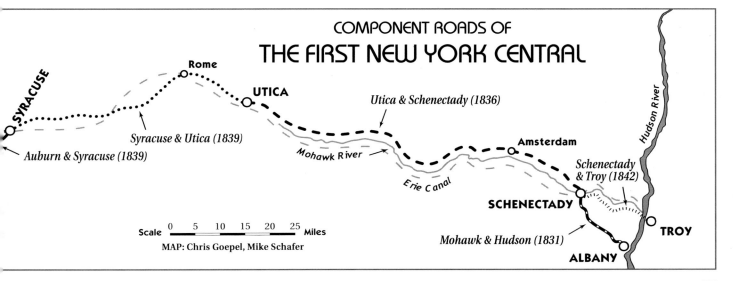

COMPONENT ROADS OF
THE FIRST NEW YORK CENTRAL

Syracuse & Utica (1839)

Auburn & Syracuse (1839)

Utica & Schenectady (1836)

Mohawk River

Erie Canal

Amsterdam

Hudson River

Schenectady & Troy (1842)

SCHENECTADY

Mohawk & Hudson (1831)

TROY

ALBANY

Scale 0 5 10 15 20 25 Miles

MAP: Chris Goepel, Mike Schafer

COMMODORE VANDERBILT
(1794-1877)

More than any other, the Vanderbilt name is synonymous with New York Central history and lore. Born into a poor Dutch farming family on Staten Island, Cornelius Vanderbilt entered the transportation business when he was 17 years old and built his fortune in New York City-based marine shipping. He was a shrewd businessman, always looking for a competitor's weakness. A true maverick, he was ruthless, unyielding, and unmerciful, making the most of every opportunity. He gradually built up his marine trade, operating a growing fleet of steam ships. He was commonly known as "the Commodore," having acquired the nickname for his cunning mastery of the lucrative oyster trade during his early shipping days. He disregarded laws that didn't suit him and was notorious for strong-armed business tactics. He threatened his rivals and frequently resorted to bribery and coercion whenever he saw fit. He was quick to enlist those that might help him, and swift to crush anyone who stood in his way. Upon the realization that two of his business allies had betrayed his trust and taken advantage of him, Vanderbilt is credited as saying, "You have undertaken to cheat me. I won't sue you, for the law is too slow. I'll ruin you."

During the California Gold Rush his Accessory Transit Company transported would-be argonauts to California by way of Latin America—a trade that proved so lucrative that he celebrated by spending a year's holiday touring Europe with his family. On the eve of the Civil War, Cornelius Vanderbilt was worth a million dollars, and by the end of the war his fortune had soared to $20 million, making him among the richest men in America.

Vanderbilt had 40 years experience with marine shipping before he looked at that nouveau-American business—railroads. It is often suggested that his view of railroads had been tainted when he was involved in a serious train wreck on the Camden & Amboy (a component line of the Pennsylvania Railroad) in 1833. The carriage he was riding derailed and overturned, injuring him and killing several other passengers. Regardless, of this unfortunate event, Vanderbilt took a keener eye to railroading two decades later, yet approached the venture with caution. During the mid-1850s, Vanderbilt gradually bought interest in the New York & Harlaem (later spelled "Harlem"). In 1857 he lent the line a considerable sum of money when it suffered from financial difficulties. A few years later, during the Civil War, he decided to take the railroad business more seriously.

Vanderbilt's railroad interest was partially an extension of a feud with his arch nemesis and age-old business rival Daniel Drew, who like Vanderbilt had competed in New York-based marine shipping. When Drew had taken an interest in the New York & Erie Railroad, Vanderbilt envisioned a competing scheme that led to his long association with the NYC. Although Vanderbilt was in his late 60s at the time, his age neither deterred him from embracing the railroad business nor hindered his ability to excel in it, and his notorious business savvy quickly propelled him to the forefront of the industry. In the course of just 15 years he would change the way railroading was done and create one of the most powerful business enterprises in the United States.

As older wealthy men are often wont to do, the Commodore wanted to be remembered. When he proposed building a huge monument to George Washington in New York City's Central Park, his wife's minister suggested it would be more beneficial to endow a university. He gave a million dollars to Central University in Nashville, Tennessee, which then changed its name to Vanderbilt University. Concerned that the NYC's fortunes might ebb following his death, he arranged in his will for the bulk of his estate to go to his son William Henry and then his grandsons so that NYC management would continued uninterrupted. And it did.

—Brian Solomon, with Jim Mischke

the route that are still served by commuter trains now operated by Metro-North Commuter Railroad.

Cornelius Vanderbilt, a name long synonymous with the New York Central, entered his illustrious career in railroading through the NY&H. Living in New York City, Vanderbilt was readily familiar with the Harlem before he decided to invest in the operation, in part to compete with age-old business rival Daniel Drew, who had acquired an interest in the New York & Erie. The Erie built westward from the Hudson River across the Southern Tier of New York to the Lake Erie port of Dunkirk, reaching there in 1851.

When Vanderbilt finally looked to control the NY&H in the 1850s, he met with resistance perpetrated by his old enemy Drew, who foresaw the Commodore's intentions and tried to foil his plans. Using his skill as a stock manipulator, Vanderbilt prevailed over Drew as he would again and again during his railroad career. Gaining control of the Harlem was the first step in Vanderbilt's scheme to reach Lake

Erie. The Commodore then placed his son, William Henry Vanderbilt, in charge of the Harlem—a move that set up the Vanderbilt's New York Central dynasty, which would extend over several generations—and went on to the next step in his quest.

HUDSON RIVER RAILROAD

Running essentially parallel to the Harlem but on a different course was the Hudson River Railroad, a comparative latecomer in the scheme of New York State railroading but a serious competitor to the Harlem—and a key component in Vanderbilt's new railroad strategies.

The mighty Hudson River had served as a main commercial thoroughfare for well over a century before the first railroads were conceived. By the 1840s, communities along the river were served by five different steamship companies, including those operated by Commodore Vanderbilt and Daniel Drew. The earliest railroads, such as the pioneering Mohawk & Hudson, terminated on the shores of the

What began as a horse-drawn city line in Manhattan in the 1830s grew to be a critical piece of Vanderbilt's early railroading endeavors in New York City. Eventually, the New York & Harlem would stretch 129 miles north from Manhattan to Chatham, New York. The Harlem would become a particularly important commuter route on the NYC, though freight is the subject of this 1938 view at Katonah, New York, on the old NY&H. *H. W. Pontin, collection of Herbert H. Harwood Jr.*

The Hudson River Railroad's river-hugging main line was surveyed by John B. Jervis and was often used by railroad photographers portraying the natural splendor of the New York Central. Famous trains were posed near the tunnels and fills initially conceived of in the 1840s. In this 1963 view along the Hudson at Cold Spring, New York, the westbound *Ohio State Limited* streaks toward Albany. *Richard J. Solomon*

river and fed traffic to steamships. Initially, a railroad line along the river was not deemed necessary for commerce nor was it considered practical to build. The east shore of the Hudson is very rugged, and as a result railroad construction would be significantly more difficult. Yet, there were visions of a Hudson River line, and in the 1830s the New York & Albany was chartered to connect its namesake points. This well-intentioned scheme never got off the ground, and a decade would pass before a serious company would build a railroad along the route.

The completion of a rail route to Boston (destined to become part of the New Haven Railroad), combined with the prospect of an inland railroad (the future New York & Harlem) between New York City and Albany, greatly concerned Hudson River communities, which suffered from a total lack of effective

transportation for at least three months every winter. Communities and businesses along the railroads in Upstate New York enjoyed all-weather transportation while those along the river between Albany and New York City enjoyed only seasonal transportation, putting them at a competitive disadvantage. In 1842, concerned Poughkeepsie business interests chartered the Hudson River Railroad. The railroad hired John B. Jervis, the well-respected engineer who had initiated several pioneer projects including the Mohawk & Hudson.

Despite Jervis' expertise, progress on the Hudson line was slow, as it was hindered by numerous natural barriers and political opposition from riverboat operators, the NY&H, and wealthy land owners along the river who did not want a railroad to spoil their view of the river valley. Jervis skillfully laid out the line along the shore of the river, using numerous cuts, fills and the occasional tunnel to maintain a nearly gradeless water-level profile. When countered with concerns about the railroad spoiling the natural splendor of the river, Jervis' spin was that it would actually improve the look of the river by smoothing out the coarseness of the shore and giving it a more symmetrical appearance that would add to its beauty. In later years the lower Hudson would be cherished as one of the scenic highlights of New York Central's "Water Level Route."

Jervis recognized the value of double track and understood the great expense involved to re-engineer a line after the initial work had been done. So, from the beginning he designed the route for double track and even made provisions for additional tracks, correctly anticipating the great traffic volume the line might handle in the future.

After nearly seven years, the railroad had only built some 40 miles, from New York City to Peekskill, arriving there in 1849. At the end of that year the first trains arrived in Poughkeepsie, nearly 73 miles, and in 1851 the railroad finally reached Albany, 142 miles, just in time to take advantage of the increase in railroad freight traffic caused by the rescinding of canal tolls imposed upon the central New York lines—and it beat the competing Harlem Line to the Albany area by just a few months. Following Jervis' advice, the entire route was double tracked within a few years of completion.

In the early years of the Hudson River Railroad, passenger service consisted of six round trips daily between New York and Albany. Connecting service was offered with the New York Central providing 18-hour timings between New York and Buffalo—exceptionally swift for the 1850s.

Despite the opening of the Hudson Line all the way to Albany and fairly robust traffic during the winter, the line suffered from anemic financial performance in its early years. Initially there was no railroad bridge across the Hudson River at Albany, and the bulk of New York City-bound railroad traffic from the west was transferred to river steamers most of the year and only relied upon the Hudson River Railroad during the winter. The rest of the year, the Hudson competed for traffic with both river boats and the NY&H, driving down rates and, consequentially, the line's profits.

Vanderbilt took an interest in the HRRR about the same time took he gained control of the NY&H, and by 1867 he controlled both and no doubt was eyeing Erastus Corning's New York Central as well. Corning had resisted Vanderbilt's early business ventures, however Corning had made many enemies within the company and aggravated shippers and stockholders alike with his archaic views toward railroading. He insisted on sending the bulk of traffic down the Hudson River and refused bridge the river at Albany despite the obvious need for one to reach the railroad's ideal eastern rail connection. In 1864 Corning resigned, and his successor completed a bridge in 1866. By this time the NYC was relying upon the Hudson River Railroad to forward its traffic in the winter only, an arrangement advantageous to the Central, but disagreeable to the HRRR, which wanted connecting traffic year-round. Vanderbilt used this grievance to his advantage, forcing the issue during the winter of 1867 after he had taken control of both all-rail routes to New York City. He waited until the Hudson was frozen, and then without warning he discontinued his direct connection with NYC, refusing to accept Central's traffic for interchange. A popular anecdote portrays that

The amalgamation of the New York Central, the Hudson River Railroad, and the New York & Harlem resulted in the New York Central & Hudson River Railroad. A turn-of-the-century scene at Cayuga, New York, just west of Auburn on the "Auburn Road" (the old Auburn & Syracuse and Auburn & Rochester lines), reveals a westbound train approaching a substantial brick water tower along Cayuga Lake, one of Upstate New York's Finger Lakes. *Mike Schafer collection*

N. Y. Central & Hudson River Railroad Station and Water Tank, Cayuga, N. Y.

A 1958 view looking due east across the Hudson River from Palisades State Park in New Jersey shows famous Spuyten Duyvil (Dutch, loosely translated as "to spite the devil"), the head of the Harlem River and a noteworthy junction point on the NYC. In 1871, Vanderbilt constructed the Spuyten Duyvil & Port Morris Railroad from this point east and south along the Harlem River to link the Hudson River Railroad with the New York & Harlem. This little connecting railroad allowed passenger trains off the HRRR to reach the new Grand Central Depot, which was located on the NY&H. The HRRR south of Spuyten Duyvil thus became primarily a freight route later known as the West Side Freight Line. In this scene, a southbound freight is crossing the Harlem River at the start of its trip down the West Side Line. *Hank Goerke*

the old Commodore suddenly refused to let his trains cross the Hudson, forcing passengers to make their way across the river to the NYC on their own, inspiring visions of bewildered passengers wading through knee deep snow carrying heavy trunks upon their backs. Outraged with this inexplicable development, people demanded an explanation. Vanderbilt innocently cited an obscure, little-known law drafted years earlier that prohibited trains of the Hudson River Railroad from crossing its namesake. He apologized, shrugging his shoulders, adding that he did not want to break the law.

Regardless of the particulars, the result from Vanderbilt's embargo was that NYC's traffic backed up at Albany, and the company

quickly began to lose business. Customers screamed, and the railroad's stock plummeted. In the mid 1860s when it had dropped low enough, Vanderbilt swiftly acquired controlling interest in the NYC and by 1867 had assumed the presidency himself. In 1869, he merged the Hudson River Railroad and New York Central, and leased the Harlem to the new company which was now called the New York Central & Hudson River Railroad.

VANDERBILT CONTROL

Central's Vanderbilt era would be marked by virtual continuous expansion through line acquisitions, mergers, and new construction as well as by improvements to the existing

railroad. Vanderbilt had the sense and resources to improve his property, which clearly set him apart from many of his contemporaries in the financial world. Although Vanderbilt was skilled at the art of stock manipulation, he was in the transportation business and recognized the value of a well-run company. Whereas some financial artists of the period looked only to buy and sell railroads as a short-term method of reaping a profit (not unlike some modern-day rail business ventures), Vanderbilt was in the game long term. He was establishing a railroad dynasty and closely involved his son William, who largely handled the day-to-day details of railroad operations.

One of the Vanderbilts' early improvements was the construction of a large new freight terminal, complete with an enormous three-story freight house, at St. Johns Park on the Hudson River Railroad in Manhattan. The front of the building featured a great bronze statue of the Commodore in the fashion of an European monarch. They had scarcely completed this project when they embarked on the construction of the first Grand Central, opened at at 42nd Street in 1871. So that passenger trains off the NYC&HR could reach the new terminal, which was on the NY&H, a connecting line was built from the Hudson Line at Spuyten Duyvil (where the Harlem River leaves the Hudson) along the Harlem River to a connection with the NY&H at Mott Haven. This allowed Harlem freight trains to reach St. Johns Park and Hudson Line passenger trains to serve Grand Central.

The consolidation led to improved schedules and better train coordination. Traffic swelled, and soon the Vanderbilts were expanding their traffic capacity with the construction of a four-track main line to Buffalo. In those primitive days of railroad operations before the advent of automatic block signaling and other traffic-control devices, adding more tracks was the best way to increase a route's capacity.

The New York Central & Hudson River Railroad had become a powerful force in American transportation, but the Vanderbilts were not content to rest on the laurels of a high-speed, four-track railroad between New York and Buffalo. Expansion became a keynote for the remainder of the nineteenth century.

Big Four Depot, Kenton, Ohio.

The "System" in New York Central System was a subtle indication that the railroad was really comprised of several smaller carriers, notably the Boston & Albany, Michigan Central, New York Central, Pittsburgh & Lake Erie, and the Cleveland, Cincinnati, Chicago & St. Louis—the "Big Four." This separate-but-equal arrangement lasted throughout most of the life of the New York Central System. The Big Four was the second-largest of the major component railroads, blanketing Ohio and Indiana and reaching through Illinois to St. Louis. Kenton, Ohio, shown early in the twentieth century, was on the Toledo–Cincinnati main line. *David P. Oroszi collection*

CENTRAL'S FAMILY GROWS

Component Railroads of the New York Central System

In the 1860s, the broad-gauge New York & Erie Railroad, which traversed New York State and connected with lines to the west, was embroiled in a three-way rate war with the New York Central and the Pennsylvania. Commodore Vanderbilt disliked competition—particularly that from Daniel Drew who controlled the Erie—so soon after Vanderbilt secured the NYC in 1864, he tried to seize the Erie as well. Although a master of stock manipulation and deceptive business practices, Vanderbilt met his match. Drew and his capable lieutenants, Jim Fisk and Jay Gould, were wise to the Commodore's schemes. They eluded his grasp through clever antics and trickery that included counterfeit stocks, an elusive game of cat-and-mouse (escaping arrest for illegal business practices in New York by sneaking over to New Jersey), and blatant bribery of elected officials and police. Finally Vanderbilt acquiesced and gave up on the Erie and instead pursued more valuable NYC interests: connections west of Buffalo. The impetus for westward expansion was the growing market in the Midwest and the rapidly expanding gateways at Cincinnati, St. Louis, and—most importantly—Chicago. Furthermore, the Vanderbilts recognized that the Pennsylvania Railroad, which by the late 1860s had already secured sound westward connections, was more serious competition then the Erie.

Long before Vanderbilt had interest in the NYC, Erastus Corning had recognized the value of securing western connections. Under Corning's guidance, Central had acquired interest in predecessors of what would become the Lake Shore & Michigan Southern, the Central's logical extension to Chicago. When Vanderbilt took over the NYC, the LS&MS was an established friendly connection, however it was controlled by men not sympathetic to the Vanderbilts.

While son William attended to the day-to-day affairs of running the Central, the Commodore made his plans. Slowly, so as not to arouse any of his adversaries' attention, he bought up stock in the LS&MS—oddly enough assisted, indirectly, by arch enemies Jay Gould and Jim Fisk. The irrepressible rascals were always on the alert for any way to make a fast million, so in 1869 they cornered the gold market, ruining many a millionaire—one of whom held enough stock in the LS&MS to have a controlling interest. Hearing of that man's need for fast cash, Vanderbilt offered him $10 million dollars for his shares—just enough to cover the fellow's loss in the gold market, though hardly what the railroad was worth. After the deal was closed, the Commodore promptly made his son-in-law, Horace Clark, the new president of the LS&MS, yet another loyal family member of his large clan and one of son William's staunchest allies in the drive to extend the NYC from Buffalo to Chicago.

The LS&MS grew from a myriad of merging companies that dated from as early as 1837. When the Lake Shore & Michigan Southern emerged following the 1869 merger of the Lake Shore Railroad, Cleveland & Toledo, and Michigan Southern & Northern Indiana, the railroad stretched between Buffalo and Chicago (reached in 1852) via Ashtabula, Cleveland, Elyria, Sandusky, and Toledo, Ohio, and Elkart and South Bend, Indiana. From Ashtabula a

A high-stepping American-type (4-4-0) locomotive hammers through Ceylon, Ohio, with an express train on the Lake Shore & Michigan Southern circa 1900. *Jay Williams collection*

branch ran south to Youngstown, Ohio, and another to Oil City, Pennsylvania. At Elyria the line split, with the northern route to Toledo passing through Sandusky while the southern route ran via Fremont to Toledo. Lines from Toledo ran north to Detroit and northwest to Jackson, Michigan. A Fort Wayne (Indiana)-to-Lansing (Michigan) line with a branch to Ypsilanti, Michigan, crossed the Toledo–South Bend main at Waterloo, Indiana. At Elkhart a branch ran north to Grand Rapids via White Pigeon and Kalamazoo. At Chicago, the Lake Shore shared terminal facilities at La Salle Street Station with the Rock Island.

THE MICHIGAN CENTRAL

Securing the Michigan Central and its Canada Southern ally—together another prime route west from the Buffalo/Niagara Falls area—took considerably longer than did the LS&MS. Initially, the Central coordinated operations with the Great Western Railway through southern Ontario to Windsor (across the river from Detroit). After a failed attempt to secure the GW, Vanderbilt instead acquired

the parallel—and bankrupt—Canada Southern in 1876. The Commodore next set his sights on the Michigan Central. Although the president of the MC was open to the idea of ownership by the Vanderbilts, he placed a high enough price on it that the Commodore was forced to buy up stock, one share at a time, rather than pay a premium price for an outright purchase. Not until 1878 did the Central gain a controlling interest in the MC, an event the Commodore never lived to see, having died in 1877. Son William merged the CS into the MC in 1882, and now the Central had a alternate route between Buffalo and Chicago that served Detroit.

Central's connection between the United States and Canada at Niagara Falls was its famous Suspension Bridge. One of the engineering marvels of its day, even the fastest trains over the road were stopped on the bridge during daylight hours so that passengers could enjoy the view thus afforded of the magnificent falls.

By 1890, the MC stretched from Buffalo west through southern Ontario over the vastly improved ex-CS via St. Thomas. Such a well-built stretch of easily graded railroad allowed trains to roll at speeds better than 60 miles per hour for the entire run to Detroit. West of Detroit the MC passed through Ann Arbor, Jackson, Battle Creek, and Kalamazoo to Niles. From Niles the main line ran west and southwest to Kensington, Illinois, via Porter (intersection with the LS&MS), Gary, and Hammond, Indiana. At Kensington on Chicago's South Side, MC trains entered Illinois Central trackage rights to reach downtown Chicago.

From Detroit, MC had a line that went north all the way to the straits of Mackinac and south to Toledo, parallel to LS&MS's Toledo–Detroit line. From Jackson, MC branches went north to Bay City and northwesterly to Grand Rapids. From Kalamazoo, branches went north to Grand Rapids, northwest to South Haven, and south to Elkart. An MC branch south out of Niles tapped the LS&MS main line at South Bend, Ind., while another ran northwesterly from South Bend to St. Joseph, Michigan. At Gary, a branch headed west to Joliet, Illinois, the westernmost point on the MC and an important connection with the Rock Island. By 1916 the New York Central owned 94 percent of the MC's capital stock.

BOSTON & ALBANY

As noted in the first chapter, New York City had greatly benefitted by the construction of the Erie Canal. Boston interests considered building a canal across Massachusetts to reach the Hudson River and the Erie Canal, but the great cost of building a waterway over the Berkshire Mountains precluded any serious interest and turned attention to railways. In 1831, three railroads were chartered in Massachusetts: the Boston & Lowell, the Boston & Providence, and, most importantly, the Boston & Worcester whose founders' goal was to reach across the state to the Hudson River.

Construction began on the B&W in August 1832 and worked its way west from Boston, reaching Newton, seven miles, in April 1834. Tracks reached Worcester, 45 miles, on July

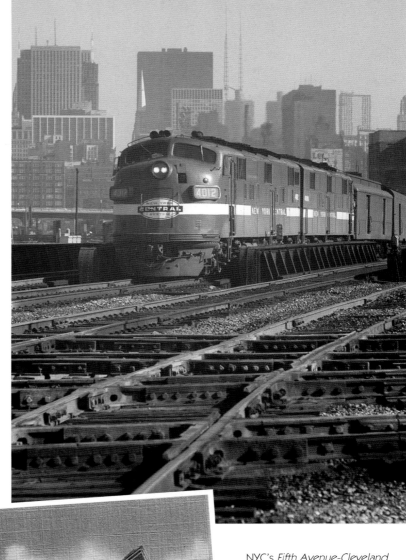

NYC's *Fifth Avenue-Cleveland Limited* departs Chicago for New York on a hazy morning in the summer of 1967. With the control of the Lake Shore & Michigan Southern established circa 1870, the New York Central & Hudson River in effect reached Chicago. *Mike Schafer*

The LS&MS shared facilities at Chicago with the Chicago, Rock Island & Pacific and the Nickel Plate. In 1903 this depot was opened at La Salle and Van Buren Streets on the south end of Chicago's Loop. It would outlast the NYC by nearly two decades. The backside of this depot is visible in the above photo, just to the left of the locomotive nose. *Mike Schafer collection*

27

3, 1835, and the following day, there was a gala celebration in Worcester combining the arrival of the railroad with Independence Day. The B&W prospered and constructed a number of short branches to reach communities near, but not on, its main line including Saxonville, Newton Lower Falls, Milford, and Brookline Village. By 1843 traffic warranted construction of a second main track.

In March 1833, two years before the B&W reached Worcester, the railroad's directors had incorporated the Western Railroad to build west from Worcester through Springfield and over the rugged Berkshires to the New York State line. There, the railroad would connect with a line building east from the Hudson River valley. Compared to the relatively swift progress of the B&W, construction of the Western was lethargic in its early years, and it was further delayed by the panic of 1837.

The railroad hired as its chief engineer Major George Washington Whistler, one of the most respected railway engineers of his generation. A graduate of West Point, he had worked on a early survey of the Baltimore & Ohio. Whistler had then gone on to work for the Boston & Lowell and later the New York, Providence & Boston. The Western proved to be one of Whistler's greatest railway challenges. Prior to its construction, most railways in both England and America adhered to fairly level profiles. In areas where steep grades were encountered, railroads employed inclined planes (such as those on the Mohawk & Hudson) rather than extended "adhesion" grades. Deviating from conventional practice, Whistler designed the Western as a continuous adhesion railroad despite some long, steeply graded sections. Furthermore, he insisted, against protests from Western's directors, that the entire line be graded for double track.

Working west from Worcester, Whistler encountered several formidable crossings. The first steep grade was up over Charlton Hill, whose summit was 57 miles from Boston. From Charlton, the railroad gradually descended through the Quaboag River valley through Palmer to Springfield in the Connecticut River valley. Once across that river, the railroad began a gradual climb into the Berkshire foothills. At Chester the railroad began its steepest ascent. From Chester he laid out the line to a summit at Washington, elevation 1,459 feet above sea level, by following the West Branch of the Westfield River. The railroad featured a 1.67 ruling grade and used the longest continuous adhesion grade of any line built up until that time. The rough terrain in the Berkshires forced Whistler to dig numerous cuts through the stone, using black powder and gangs of men with pick axes. Whistler crossed the river a dozen times, often bridging it on huge stone-arch bridges constructed of cut granite blocks.

The Michigan Central blanketed its namesake state. MC's principal mainline route in Michigan was that between Detroit and Chicago via Jackson, Kalamazoo, and Niles— today's Amtrak route— however there was an alternate route between Jackson and Niles via Three Rivers. In the turn-of-the-century scene below, an MC train calls are Vandalia, Michigan, on the Three Rivers line. *Mike Schafer collection*

Whistler's superb engineering paid off. Today his right-of-way remains one of the lowest crossings of the Berkshires, several hundred feet lower than the parallel Massachusetts Turnpike would build more than 110 years later. With the exception of a few short line changes, the railroad still adheres to Whistler's profile.

The Western opened to Springfield in 1839 and reached the state line in 1841. There, the Western met the Hudson & Berkshire, a shoddily constructed line that ran east from the village of Hudson, New York, on the bank of its namesake river some 30 miles south of Albany. Later, the Albany & West Stockbridge supplanted the H&B, using a better-engineered line direct to Albany via the short, curved State Line Tunnel located a mile or so west of the New York-Massachusetts state line.

The Western was the world's first mountain railroad. Whistler ordered special locomotives for the task of moving trains over mountains: a fleet of vertical-boiler 0-8-0s designed for slow speed and very high tractive effort. At a time when most locomotives used only one set of drivers, these curious beasts, known as "mud diggers," each employed four sets of drivers.

Whistler remains a little-known figure, but his son James became an internationally known artist, best known for a painting which portrays his mother in a rocking chair. Today some of George Whistler's bridges survive, although most are unused relics, abandoned by the NYC when it straightened the railroad between Chester and Middlefield.

In 1867, as Commodore Vanderbilt was consolidating his properties, the B&W and Western finally were merged, forming the Boston & Albany. Prior to these post-Civil War consolidations, Western's president Chester Chapin established close ties

Michigan Central's headquarters were housed in this depot/ office building near downtown Detroit. The structure towered over a coach yard and locomotive servicing facility, as illustrated in this 1953 view. Note that the Detroit River Tunnel electrification was still in use, as evidenced by the third-rail distribution system and the electric switcher working the coach yard at left. Elmer Treloar, collection of Herbert H. Harwood Jr.

29

Of all of New York Central System's family roads, the Boston & Albany retained the staunchest independence, its steam locomotive fleet lettered for the B&A right up to the end. Even in the 1990s, Conrail's line between Albany and Boston was referred to by crews as "the B&A." Here in August 1947, a B&A suburban 4-6-6T tank engine is at Trinity Place station in Boston. *Ollie Fife, collection of Herbert H. Harwood Jr.*

between his railroad and the Central. He would serve on the NYC's board and later became an associate of Vanderbilt.

Although the B&A did not assemble a vast network of intertwining branches and secondary main lines like the two other large New England systems, the Boston & Maine and the New York, New Haven & Hartford, it did add some feeders to its main route as well as a line from Pittsfield to North Adams, Massachusetts. In 1873 the B&A acquired the Ware River Line extending from Palmer up to Winchendon, and in 1880 it bought a 48-mile line running from Springfield northeast to Athol, Massachusetts. B&A also built a branch south from Worcester to Webster and operated short branches nearby to Spencer, and North Brookfield. In suburban Boston, B&A developed its Highland branch as a commuter loop during the mid-1880s. This sinuous roller coaster line ran south of the main line through Newton connecting with the main line at both ends.

In 1880 the B&A and NYC signed a joint traffic agreement for through movements, and

in 1900 Central cemented its long-time relationship with the B&A by leasing the railroad. NYC control resulted in numerous improvements to the property, notably better coordination of both freight and passenger services. Central invested in the B&A by upgrading physical plant, adding a second bore to State Line Tunnel, and installing several long sections of third main track and sidings to improve traffic flow.

One area of contention that came with NYC control was the loss of Boston & Albany lettering on equipment. This annoyed people who held a fierce regional loyalty to the B&A, and eventually the Central yielded to these sentiments and restored B&A lettering on equipment regularly assigned to the railroad—a policy that remained through the end of the steam era. On April 3, 1961—nearly ten years after the last B&A steam locomotive had made its last run on home rails—the B&A was merged into the New York Central. Despite this technicality, B&A signage survived well into the Conrail era, and many people—

employees and public alike—still refer to former Boston & Albany lines as the "B&A." No reference is made to its one-time lessor.

THE NEW YORK, CHICAGO & ST. LOUIS

Though usually thought of as a rival to New York Central, the New York, Chicago & St. Louis—better known as the Nickel Plate—was once a component of the far-flung NYC. Incorporated in Indiana in February 1881, the NYC&StL was run by two of the shrewdest men to ever do battle with the Vanderbilts, and to this day historians argue whether the reason the road existed had more to do with the backers' intentions to sell it off or operate it.

In 1871 Charles Foster and Calvin Brice were traipsing through the countryside selling bonds for the insolvent Lake Erie & Louisville, which was building west from Fremont, Ohio, into Indiana. By 1876 they were president and vice president of same. The speed of their rise to the top was enhanced by some clever manipulation of the ballot box at a shareholders meeting attended by the pair and no one else. The new officers were quick to spot an opportunity to expand the line and joined forces with New York City banker George Seney and his associates. Consolidating a cadre of fledgling railroads, including the LE&L, they formed the Lake Erie & Western in 1879, running from Findlay, Ohio, to Bloomington, in central Illinois, and began laying rails northeast to Lake Erie at a furious pace. In the winter of 1880-81, the rails arrived in Sandusky, Ohio, aided by that community's monies—Seney and company having looted the till. A deal was struck with Vanderbilts' Lake Shore & Michigan Southern to interchange freight and passengers at Sandusky.

Shortly a dispute arose between the LE&W and the LS&MS, and management of the former decided to build their own line west to Cleveland and Chicago and east to Buffalo. The result

was the New York, Chicago & St. Louis, formed in 1881 with the money from a ton of watered stock. Amazingly, the Nickel Plate was up and running in 1882, 500 miles from Buffalo to Chicago. No terminal existed in either Chicago or Buffalo, but the stage was set, and Brice wasted no time courting Erie's Jay Gould and Lake Shore's William Vanderbilt.

Since most of the capital for the line had gone into the pockets of Brice and Seney, the Nickel Plate was now close to insolvency, but it was too much of a plum—albeit a shriveled one—for Vanderbilt to ignore, and he invested heavily in NKP stock. The thought of Gould's Erie controlling the line was too bleak a prospect considering his own investment in the Lake Shore. Vanderbilt promptly offered ownership of the stock to the directors of the Lake Shore; they accepted, and he just as

BELOW: An early view of Springfield (Massachusetts) station shared by B&A, New Haven, and Boston & Maine. *Robert A. Buck collection*

BOTTOM: A postcard scene from the turn of the century shows the original B&A right-of-way near Middlefield, Massachusetts. *Michael Sullivan collection*

View near Middlefield, Mass.

quickly loaned the failing road $2 million to shore it up. Brice and Seney left the playing field with a satchel full of money, and Vanderbilt had yet another railroad to Chicago, which the Central operated principally as an alternate freight route.

Despite Vanderbilt's cash infusion, the Nickel Plate went into receivership in 1885 and was reorganized by 1887. By this time Brice was still happily running his LE&W and was always looking to add more mileage to it, which he did through acquisition of several other railroads. By 1890 the L&EW boasted 848 route-miles. After a term as a U.S. senator, Brice died suddenly in 1898 at the age of 53.

By 1899 the NYC had bought over 100,000 shares of LE&W stock. In 1916, under pressure from the Interstate Commerce Commission, the Central happily sold its stock in the perennial money-losing Nickel Plate to Cleveland's Van Sweringen brothers. Then in 1922, the Central sold its LE&W stock to the Van Sweringens, who happily added it to their growing Nickel Plate empire—now headed for St. Louis. With a main line from Buffalo to Chicago and from Cleveland and Toledo to St. Louis, the Nickel Plate became a worthy competitor to the NYC in those corridors during the twentieth century.

TOLEDO & OHIO CENTRAL

The coal fields of southeastern Ohio had been opened up by 1868, and the deposits along the length of the Sunday Creek Valley were the impetus for the Atlantic & Lake Erie, chartered in 1869 to run from Toledo to Pomeroy, Ohio, on the Ohio River, but bypassing Columbus to the east. Only seven miles of track were actually built under the A&LE banner, wheezing along southeast from New Lexington, only to dead-end at an incomplete tunnel at Moxahala. Reorganized and renamed Ohio Central in 1876, a receiver was appointed in 1878 to sell it off.

At which point we find the able Messrs. Calvin Brice, Charles Foster, and a new set of cronies listed as stockholders of the Columbus & Sunday Creek Valley Railroad. Buying the completed part of the line between Moxahala and New Lexington, they finished the tunnel and pushed a new line north 57 miles to Columbus. Despite the high cost of completing the tunnel, the line's prospects seemed secure, and the remainder of the OC charter was purchased from the receiver. The originally proposed line between Toledo and Middleport/Pomeroy by way of Mount Gilead was built by 1882. Now, Brice and company convinced the principals of two other lines, the Atlantic & Northwestern and the Richmond & Allegheny, to sell out to the OC. The A&N was more a proposal than anything, aimed at crossing the Ohio River to reach Charleston, West Virginia. The R&A connected the Virginia cities of Richmond and Clifton Forge.

As the Richmond, Allegheny & Ohio Central, this new amalgamation (with some gaps to be filled in) would feature ports at Richmond and Toledo and coal fields in between, thus ensuring coal traffic headed both east and west—a dependable source of revenue if there ever was one. Unfortunately for the RA&OC, the Virginia Legislature denied the R&A's entry into the union. Without an Eastern tidewater port, the RA&OC foundered and went into receivership in 1883.

Despite its declining fortunes, the line was extended to Charleston and the surrounding coal fields as intended. By 1885 car loadings had improved, and the line, renamed the Toledo & Ohio Central, was on the rebound. During 1892 the T&OC bought the Toledo, Columbus & Cincinnati, which was slowly building south from Toledo to Columbus via Kenton. The T&OC completed the line from Kenton to Columbus in 1893 where it was connected with the old OC branch that had been extended up from New Lexington years earlier. The T&OC now had essentially two routes between the Ohio River and Toledo.

Though almost never associated with West Virginia, the New York Central nonetheless served that state through its Toledo & Ohio Central lines. By having its own artery into coal country—a critical factor during railroading's steam era—Central avoided being held hostage by coal interests. *Mike Schafer collection*

The T&OC prospered and by 1922 traffic was such that it was leased by the Central. In 1938, the T&OC was merged into the New York Central System.

PITTSBURGH & LAKE ERIE

During the railroad boom of the 1870s, the Pittsburgh & Lake Erie was incorporated to build a railroad from Pittsburgh down the Ohio River and then up the Mahoning River to Youngstown, Ohio. Promoted by steel-industry magnate Andrew Carnegie, the line drew the attention of John Newell, general manager of Vanderbilts' Lake Shore & Michigan Southern. Newell had made his reputation as a forward-thinking man and saw the P&LE as Central's opportunity to tap the valley's potential for traffic, thanks to the region's numerous steel mills. By 1878 the railroad was under construction; operations began during 1879. An extension southeast to Connellsville was built by the Vanderbilts on Mr. Newell's advice and finished by 1883.

By 1884, the Lake Shore held such sway in P&LE affairs that Newell became the president of the line—and what a line it was. In 1907 the 123-mile railroad had such a large concentration of heavy shippers that it earned $100,000 a mile or more for many consecutive quarters. Paying a 12 percent dividend that year, the entire main line was four-tracked to further facilitate the speedy movement of the torrent of freight produced by on-line shippers. Traditionally, it came to be that the P&LE president and the NYC president were one in the same, a custom that continued into the 1960s.

Interestingly, the P&LE was never fully merged into the NYC. Not only did the P&LE outlive the NYC, but also NYC successors Penn Central and Conrail. Today the P&LE remains an independent carrier.

THE BEACH CREEK RAILROAD AND THE FALL BROOK LINE

Central's "invasion" of Pennsylvania Railroad and Erie Railroad territory in northern and central Pennsylvania was done to protect its source of motive-power fuel. In the late

1880s coal-mine owners upped the per-ton price of coal shipped on the Central by fifty cents, raising the ire of Central management in general and William H. Vanderbilt in particular. With no on-line coal shippers more or less in the pocket of the Vanderbilts, the NYC was in effect being held hostage to the marketplace and forced to pay the increase. The net result was an increase in the cost of steam-locomotive operations; future increases loomed.

NYC management set out to find a source of coal that could be bought to hedge the cost of engine fuel and would be convenient to the railroad's center of operations (rival PRR was already well ensconced in coal country). Vanderbilt's first hedge was the purchase of a large block of stock in the Philadelphia & Reading, a line strategically positioned in the Schuylkill coal fields of southeastern Pennsylvania—and a competitor of arch enemy PRR.

By this time William Vanderbilt's sons, Cornelius II and William K., were in charge of the NYC and had invested in the McIntyre Coal Company north of Williamsport, Pennsylvania. They reorganized and revamped McIntyre by infusing their capital as well as that of such newly moneyed men as Samuel Clemens, better known as Mark Twain. Clemens also bought stock with the Vanderbilts in a mine reorganized as the Clearfield Bituminous Coal Company, the idea being that the Central would find a home for Clearfield coal in the fireboxes of its locomotives. The Clearfield's

NYC-painted locomotives were common on P&LE lines, but P&LE equipment was so lettered and some diesels carried a separate P&LE paint scheme as illustrated by the locomotive at left in this 1962 photo at McKees Rocks, Pennsylvania. *Lou Marre*

Beech Creek Railroad ran west from Jersey Shore through the Clearfield coal district and eventually met the Lake Shore & Michigan Southern's branch out of Ashtabula, Ohio, at Polk, Pennsylvania.

Another hedge was the Fall Brook Coal Company, which by 1881 had a line that ran from NYC's Auburn Road main line through Geneva, New York, south through "the Grand Canyon of Pennsylvania" to Jersey Shore and then east a short distance to Williamsport. In 1890 the NYC took out a long-term lease on the 153-mile Beech Creek Railroad, and in 1899 the Fall Brook lines became part of the system as well. The Central never again was held hostage by coal-mine operators.

THE BEE LINE AND THE BIG FOUR

The Cleveland, Columbus & Cincinnati—the genesis of the "Bee Line"—was chartered in 1836 during the rush of railroad-building enthusiasm that then gripped Ohio. Construction did not begin until 1847, however, and was slow at best. At one point in 1849, CC&C directors were so fearful that the charter

would be invalidated by the State for lack of progress that they authorized contractors to finish a 36-mile section in exchange for half the company's net profit for the next ten months! Finish they did, and by 1851 three trains were running daily each way between Cleveland and Columbus. In 1852 the line partnered up with the Little Miami Railroad and the Columbus & Xenia to form a through route between Cleveland and Cincinnati.

During 1848 both the Bellefontaine (BELL-fountin) & Indiana and the Indianapolis & Bellefontaine were incorporated in the State of Ohio to connect Galion, Ohio, and Indianapolis, Indiana. Construction on the B&I was completed in 1853. In 1863 the B&I and I&B merged and the resulting Bellefontaine Railroad became known as the "B Line." Later the company adopted the phrase "Bee Line" in its advertising, and when the CC&C took the Bellefontaine into the fold in 1868 the nickname stuck, and the resulting Cleveland, Columbus, Cincinnati & Indianapolis Railroad was known as the Bee Line for the next 21 years.

Next was the Big Four. Its infancy can be traced to the spring of 1880 and the financial wreckage of the Cincinnati & Indiana, the Indianapolis, Cincinnati & Lafayette, and the Cincinnati, Lafayette & Chicago. Out of their ashes arose the new Cincinnati, Indianapolis,

A Big Four timetable from 1939 featured Cincinnati Union Terminal, served by Big Four trains to and from Chicago, Cleveland, and New York. *Mike Schafer collection*

The Big Four's ponderous depot at Bellefontaine, Ohio, circa 1910. This was a division point on the railroad and a Big Four shop complex. *David P. Oroszi collection*

St. Louis & Chicago Railroad—the first "Big Four." The CIStL&C ran from from Cincinnati, Ohio, northwest through Indianapolis and Lafayette, Indiana, to Kankakee, Illinois. From there it used Illinois Central tracks to reach Chicago. "Big four" references the cities in the railroad's name, but just how the Big Four nickname came into use remains a mystery. There are a number of stories, a favorite being that of the lazy clerk who, tired of writing the railroad's long name on the timetable blackboard, coined the Big Four moniker supposedly to save chalk!

In 1881 the line was still in receivership, but under the talented and resourceful eye of Melville E. Ingalls the road slowly recovered from the excesses of prior management. Young Ingalls, only 28 years old, had been a lawyer before he became a state senator for Massachusetts. Having served the state brilliantly, he attracted the attention of certain Eastern bankers who had invested heavily in the Big Four's ill-fated predecessor lines, and they brought him in to run the new railroad. Ingalls had scant resources with which to work, but work he did, and the new line slowly showed the benefits of his prudence.

Working jointly with the Chicago, Rock Island & Pacific, the CIStL&C in 1881 was extended west from Kankakee to Seneca, Illinois, on the Illinois River where connection was made with the Rock Island's main line west from Chicago thus forming a bypass around Chicago's congestion. Another interesting development that same year was the appearance of Collis P. Huntington—of Southern Pacific and Chesapeake & Ohio fame—on the Big Four's board of directors.

Meanwhile the Vanderbilts were sizing up the Big Four as a possible western connection for the NYC. They wasted no time in buying up a large block of stock, and in 1889 they merged the Bee Line with the Big Four, making the "second" Big Four—the Cleveland, Cincinnati, Chicago & St. Louis Railroad—with Ingalls at the helm. In addition they bought the "Egyptian line" between Cairo and Danville, Illinois, in 1884, renaming it the Cairo, Vincennes & Chicago to reflect a goal of reaching Lake Michigan. The St. Louis, Alton & Terre Haute Railroad, serving its namesake cities, was also purchased about this time. The line from Danville north to Indiana Harbor, between Gary and Chicago, was completed in 1906, and

through a connection with the NYC (LS&MS) main line at Indiana Harbor, the CV&C was able to tap Chicago traffic.

Two other railroads added to the Big Four fold were the Peoria & Eastern and the Cincinnati Northern. The P&E, which ran from Pekin, Illinois, near Peoria, to Springfield, Ohio, via Indianapolis, was the result of a series of railroad amalgamations that harkened to the Mad River & Lake Erie, chartered in 1831 to build a line from Sandusky to Dayton, Ohio, via Springfield. The MR&LE eventually morphed into the Cincinnati, Sandusky & Cleveland and was acquired by the Indiana, Bloomington & Western, which ran between Springfield, Ohio, and Pekin via Indianapolis, Indiana, and Danville and Bloomington, Illinois. The newly expanded IB&W thus had a through route from Lake Erie to the central Illinois rail hub of Peoria/Pekin.

The IB&W went through a series of financial convulsions during an eleven-day period in 1887 during which it was broken into three

As with the Pennsylvania Railroad, St. Louis was the westernmost point on the New York Central System. Under the banner of Big Four, trackage actually terminated in East St. Louis, Illinois, and never reached Missouri per se, and NYC passenger trains and selected freights entered St. Louis proper on the Terminal Railroad Association. This is the *Knickerbocker* arriving St. Louis from New York City in August 1966. *Mike Schafer*

NYC's "Egyptian Line" to Carmi and Cairo, Illinois, was an unremarked piece of Big Four property stretching 370 miles from Indiana Harbor, Indiana (near Chicago) to the southernmost tip of Illinois. Train 463, the remnant of the *Egyptian*, stands at the end of its overnight run from Chicago at Harrisburg, Illinois, on April 26, 1957—possibly the last run of this train. *Lou Marre*

separate railroads and reassembled back into one—the Ohio, Indiana & Western. From the OI&W there emerged, though a complex bit of corporate foreplay, the P&E. The P&E became a profitable road and was subleased by the NYC from the Big Four in 1930. The P&E remained more or less an entity until its 1976 absorption into Conrail.

The origins of the Cincinnati Northern are not quite as convoluted. Chartered in 1881, the Cincinnati, Van Wert & Michigan began poking track north from Franklin, Ohio, its anchor point to the Bee Line near Cincinnati. It crossed the LS&MS at Bryan, Ohio, and got as far as the Michigan state line where it met the Jackson & Ohio, whose tracks ran north to

Jackson, Michigan. The two lines combined in 1886 to form the Cincinnati, Jackson & Mackinaw Railroad. During the next ten years the railroad was owned by none other than Calvin Brice, and after his death it became the property of the Cincinnati Northern, a terminal road serving Cincinnati and nearby Dayton. The Big Four purchased all the capital stock of the CN in 1902.

Melville Ingalls served as president of the Big Four until 1900 when he became the chairman of the board. That same year the NYC and the PRR joined with the Big Four in the purchase of the C&O—seemingly what Collis Huntington might have had in mind when he and Ingalls met back in 1881.

The last major railroad to be included in the Big Four, the Evansville Indianapolis & Terre Haute, was added in 1920. Ten years later the NYC leased the Big Four for 99 years.

THE WEST SHORE

By the late 1860s, the volume of traffic that was riding the rails over the Commodore's railroad from New York City north to Albany was great enough that some of his competitors began pursuing another rail route up the Hudson River. A survey along the west shore of the Hudson was made, and by 1880 the New York, West Shore & Buffalo was formed to run tracks between its namesake cities.

Starting at Weehawken, New Jersey, opposite Manhattan, the line dove into a nearly

From his vantage point on the U.S. Route 51 overpass in Bloomington, Illinois, the photographer has recorded the arrival of a chartered passenger train (possibly for an Illinois State University sports event) on the Peoria & Eastern in the late 1950s. The parallel line at left is the Nickel Plate, also once a component of the New York Central System. *Mike Schafer collection*

mile-long tunnel through the Palisades Ridge and then veered north. Following the valley up to Haverstraw, New York, the line had to bore through the ridge again to reach the banks of the Hudson whereupon it stayed until the vicinity of Albany. This Hudson-side stretch of the West Shore was a costly project, for the west bank of the Hudson proved to be a formidable adversary—nine tunnels were required as were many bridges and fills. Nonetheless, the right-of-way was built to the highest standard and of low gradient. Financed in part by rival Pennsylvania Railroad as part of its never-ending battle with the Central, no expense was spared to make the West Shore a smooth-running alternative to the NYC.

Finished by 1884, the NYWS&B began siphoning traffic off of the Central as soon as it opened. Funneling freight fed to it by disgruntled NYC customers and traffic that came up from the south through Jersey, the new West Shore boasted a slightly shorter route to Buffalo along with a fine fleet of clean, anthracite-burning engines. The downside was the West Shore's lack of a direct rail line into New York City, which instead was served by a ferry connection across the Hudson. To attract more business, passenger rates were slashed, but

the ferry crossing still proved a barrier, and rates were cut again. The West Shore began to bleed red ink, and soon the railroad—and then the contractor who built it—went into bankruptcy. The PRR had no choice but to buy more of the railroad's bonds as an attempt to stem the tide of red ink.

William Vanderbilt covered *his* West Shore-related losses from accumulated cash and began laying his plans. It seems that a railroad—the South Pennsylvania—had been chartered across Pennsylvania that, if it were built as planned, would be quite a bit shorter and of easier gradient than rival PRR's Philadelphia–Harrisburg–Pittsburgh Main Line. Vanderbilt saw the chance to strike at his arch enemy's heart. With the aid of Andrew Carnegie (whose Homestead steel plant the new route would serve) and John D. Rockefeller, Vanderbilt actually started construction of the South Pennsylvania, completing long stretches of superbly engineered right-of-way and a series of impressive tunnels and bridges.

By 1885 an alarmed J. P. Morgan, seeing the accumulated capital of both the PRR and the NYC going up in smoke (not to mention his holdings in both the companies as the stock of each plummeted) called a hurried meeting on

In 1932, at the time of this photo at Kingston, New York, the West Shore featured a full complement of passenger trains between Weehawken, New Jersey and Albany—about a half dozen each way on weekdays—plus numerous commuter runs. Some were name trains—the *Storm King* and the *West Pointer*—featuring parlor-car service. *Cal's Classics*

his yacht. It's said that as soon as the heads of both lines embarked, the hawsers were pulled on board, and the boat set sail. Morgan reasoned that none of the men would want off bad enough to jump and swim, so the grand yacht headed to the center of the Hudson River and sailed slowly north. When darkness fell, Morgan had his deal: the PRR would buy the South Pennsylvania Railroad, and the NYC would lease the West Shore after it went bankrupt. It immediately did, and in 1885 the Central signed a lease for 475 years at $2 million a year. William Vanderbilt died shortly after the lease was signed.

The West Shore matured into a valuable acquisition as a freight route, particularly south of Albany. As freight traffic declined in and out of Manhattan proper in later years, it increased on the New Jersey side of the Hudson, and the West Shore was there to accommodate. Further, the east shore main line had become passenger-intensive, which it remains to this day, and the separation of freight and passenger traffic benefitted the flow of both.

As for the South Pennsylvania Railroad, no rails were ever laid, and the PRR sold it to the State of Pennsylvania in the 1930s. Today, parts of the well-engineered right-of-way serve as the foundation of the Pennsylvania Turnpike.

CENTRAL HEADS FOR THE NORTH COUNTRY

Rails to the north country, long a desire of the locals in Rome, New York, on the main line of the New York Central & Hudson River, were a long time coming. The charter for the Watertown & Rome Railroad sat dormant for 16 years before any work on the line was accomplished other than the expelling of hot air by the promoters. Chartered in 1832, construction got underway in 1849; by 1851, 72 miles of

trackage were finished, between Rome and Watertown, New York. The little line prospered and paid a whopping 10 per cent on its bonds for many years, inspiring other companies to build either connecting or competing lines. The Potsdam & Watertown was one of the former, connecting with the R&W at Watertown and running some 70 miles northeast to Norwood, New York. There the P&W connected with the Northern Railroad (later part of the Rutland Railroad) and its connections west to Ogdensburg, New York, and east to Rouses Point, New York, to meet lines to Boston via Vermont.

In 1861 the W&R and P&W merged to form the Rome, Watertown & Ogdensburg. The new road built branches to Ogdensburg and Oswego, New York, on Lake Ontario. By 1864 the RW&O was building locomotives and freight and passenger rolling stock in its own shops at Rome.

As the fortunes of the RW&O continued to improve, the line leased the Syracuse & Northern in 1868, adding trackage from Oswego to Syracuse. In 1875 the RW&O bought the assets of the Lake Ontario Shore Railroad at that road's bankruptcy sale. The LOS ran from Oswego west to Niagara Falls, hugging the south shore of Lake Ontario most of the way. The line was intended to serve as a bridge route for traffic moving between Boston and the west via the Boston & Maine's Hoosac Tunnel line, but this traffic never materialized. It didn't help that the new line avoided the heart of Rochester and, worse, bypassed nearly all the major farming communities.

By 1878 the RW&O was in default on its bonds, and the Delaware, Lackawanna & Western bought it for a song. Under the leadership of Lackawanna President Samuel Sloan the line's fortunes continued to falter. Finally, in 1882 DL&W control was upset by a sly Connecticut Yankee with a waistcoat pocket full of proxies—and enough cash to pay back the Lackawanna monies borrowed by the RW&O. Charles Parsons took the helm and spent money on improvements. He added the Utica & Black Rivers, which ran from Utica to the St. Lawrence River and included a branch to Ogdensburg. In 1886 he also leased the Carthage, Watertown & Sacketts Harbor, another feeder of on-line freight. From the northern terminus of Norwood on the old P&W, Parsons built an extension to Massena,

What it lacked in revenues, the Putnam Division made up for in quaintness. It's about 8:30 A.M. as two-car Put train No. 104 trots into Gray Oaks, New York, on May 4, 1948 on its run to the Bronx from Yorktown Heights. *Collection of Herbert H. Harwood Jr.*

New York, connecting there with the Grand Trunk Eastern for access to traffic to and from Montreal. He also built a spur into downtown Rochester. As business improved, the price of RW&O stock rose and garnered the attention of Central's management.

NYC&HR management tried to buy up stock in the RW&O but found little to be had. Finally they located a dormant railroad charter so they could start a competing line to Watertown from a convenient point along the Central's Albany–Buffalo main line. This ploy had the desired effect. RW&O management leased the property to the NYC&HR in 1891, and in 1913 it was formally absorbed into the New York Central System.

Still another property in the North Country was the St. Lawrence & Adirondack, a narrow-gauge line that ran from Herkimer, New York (also on the NYC&HR main line) a few miles north to Poland. Purchased in 1891 by Dr. Seward Webb, William Vanderbilt's son-in-law, Webb soon had the line widened to standard gauge and running all the way through the heart of the Adirondack Mountains to Malone, New York, on the Northern Railroad. There it met another segment being constructed separately north to Montreal. Money was no object with the good doctor, and he combined all the charters of these lines into the Mohawk & Malone Railroad and began work in earnest as only a Vanderbilt heir could do. In short order, he established through sleeping-car service from New York City and Buffalo to Montreal via the scenic Adirondack line, which included a branch to Lake Placid via Saranac Lake, both popular tourist destinations. The trains of the good Doc made the trip easy. In 1902 he leased the Mohawk & Malone to the NYC and in 1905 sold all his stock in the Canadian part of the line to the NYC as well.

THE "PUT"

The 52-mile Putnam line, running between New York City and Brewster via Yonkers started out in 1869 as part of the stillborn New York & Boston, intended to link the two important cities. The NY&B evolved into the New York & Northern in 1880 and bought a little rail line that ran up to Yonkers. The NY&N caught the attention of the Reading Company's A. A. McLeod, who envisioned it as a gateway for his line to New England. Central's men lost no time buying up stock in the NY&N, beating

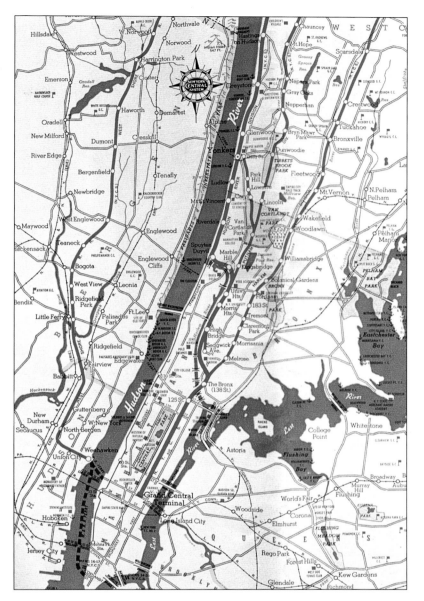

McLeod to the punch. The little line never made money regardless of who was interested in its future, and it's creditors forced a foreclosure and its resulting public sale in December 1893. J. P. Morgan himself attended, casting the first and last bid for the line; the gavel was knocked down three times to the tune of $1 million, and the railroad was his. By 1894 the railroad was officially part of the Central. The line was extended to Brewster where connection was made with the Harlem line, and it served primarily as a commuter line for the quaint towns that clung to its path. The line became NYC's Putnam Division—"The Put," as it was known locally.

A map from an NYC promotional brochure illustrates how the old Hudson River Railroad, New York & Harlem, West Shore, New York & Northern, and Spuyten Duyvil & Port Morris all were tied together to give the Central an enviable prominence in metropolitan New York. *C. W. Newton collection*

At the dawn of the twentieth century, New York Central was well on its way to becoming an American institution, much like opponent Pennsylvania Railroad. But for the railroad industry it would be a tumultuous century beset by war and depression. One bright spot would be the Century of Progress Exhibition in Chicago during 1933-34—a turning point of hope for a country in the grips of the Great Depression. A new America would rise from the Depression—and the war that followed. *C. W. Newton collection*

CENTRAL IN THE NEW CENTURY

1890-1945: Coming of Age...and Wars and Depression

By 1890 the New York Central & Hudson River and its subsidiaries had become a 10,000-mile system, operating in eleven states and two Canadian provinces, and serving more than half of the U.S. population. Employees numbered 200,000, among them some of the better-paid men and women in the region. It was claimed that the railroad paid state taxes at the rate of $150 per hour, a princely sum in those days, but testament to the sheer size of the organization and the amount of money it generated even then. Reformers of the day were even wont to say that the Central made a better life for its employees and customers than it could if it were a hundred small companies—a surprising comment, for this was the era of the rail barons and certainly the Vanderbilts could be counted among them.

During the last half of the nineteenth century, man and his machines—and the railroads—had created the greatest concentration of industrial production in the world, from Pittsburgh north to Buffalo, west to Cleveland, Detroit, and Chicago, and again north to Milwaukee: this was America's "Steel Belt." This extended region was well served by the Central and its leased affiliates. The Central was still growing, and as the economy of the American Midwest grew at a frantic pace, so did the traffic on the line.

Under the direction of Central's visionary passenger agent-turned-public relations guru, George H. Daniels, the road inaugurated new high-speed luxury train service, beginning with the 1891 launching of the Empire State Express, a fast day train between New York and Buffalo. In 1893 NYC&HR engine No. 999, a high-wheeled 4-4-0, sped the popular *Empire State Express* along at 112.5 mph between Batavia and Buffalo, capturing world attention. Hailed as the fastest locomotive on earth, the 999 was exhibited by the railroad at the great Columbian Exposition in Chicago that same year. (Today the 999 is displayed at Chicago's Museum of Science and Industry.)

Also for the Expo, Central inaugurated the *Exposition Flyer*, carded to take passengers from New York City to the Chicago fair in 20 hours—quite a ballast-scorcher. Despite the pounding these new flyers gave the rails, the Central's safety record was enviable, thanks to the pioneering work done in the design of the rails themselves by P. H. Dudley, one of Central's consulting engineers. His expertise in rail design and maintenance made possible the continued abuse by speeding locomotives. Rails were measured for wear by devices installed in a special car of Dudley's own design that traversed the main line checking for irregularities.

To the chagrin of NYC competitors, George Daniels coined the phrase "America's Greatest Railroad" for the Central. His magazines, books, and pamphlets—all beautifully illustrated—were some of the most prolific efforts of the kind. The 1896 edition of his book *Health and Pleasure on America's Greatest Railroad* was over 500 pages long.

The close of the nineteenth century was a turning point for Central. NYC President Chauncey Depew replaced Cornelius Vanderbilt II in 1898 as chairman of the board, a position he would retain until 1928. LS&MS's

Samuel Callaway became the new NYC president. Then, in 1899, Cornelius Vanderbilt II died. Although Vanderbilt influence on the Central would continue for the next half century, the death of this Vanderbilt marked the end—more or less—of railroading's "rail (or 'robber' some would say) baron" era.

LET THE CENTURY BEGIN

Although the waning years of the nineteenth century were hallmarked by rapid expansion on the Central (and most other U.S. railroads), the turn-of-the-century and the ensuing decades were more than not earmarked by refinements to existing systems. Growth in America's railroads continued, to be sure, but it was more in the form of traffic than new route construction or acquisitions.

The Central continued to expand its base of business, and the increased car loadings and passenger patronage prompted further improvements. Grand Central was remodeled in 1900, although even then it was acknowledged the structure would have to be replaced to keep up with the additional trains that increasing ridership demanded. Under Chief Engineer William J. Wilgus, the Central used the first U.S.-made 100-pound rail during a sweeping grade reduction and curve realignment of the main line in 1902, making way for a new run that year—the *20th Century Limited*, another brainchild of George Daniels.

Electrification of lines out from Manhattan began in 1903 as was the new Grand Central Terminal (see Chapter 5 for details). The mammoth electrification project was forced upon the railroad by the City of New York as a way to eliminate steam-locomotive smoke, but Wilgus realized that Grand Central's enlargement would be impossible without massive tunneling—and therefore electrification. The first electric-powered train rolled forth from Grand Central with great ceremony on September 30, 1906, although that event would be marred by the unexplained derailment of an electric-locomotive-hauled train in February 1907 in which 23 passengers were killed. The new Grand Central Terminal opened in 1913.

These post-1900 changes happened under the direction of William H. Newman, who had replaced Callaway as Central's president in 1901. Newman resigned as president in 1909 to concentrate his management skills on the Grand Central Terminal project, now in its culmination period. Newman was succeeded by William A. Brown, under whom the Central formally absorbed the Rome, Watertown & Ogdensburg. Brown retired in 1914, with Alfred Smith taking the helm. The railroad was already well into the process of formally merging the LS&MS and the NYC&HR, a mettlesome task that would change the way the railroad handled affiliate roads. To effect a true merger, the terms of the bonds that the originating company had issued had to be met—and therefore the scurrilous nature of some of the more notorious bondholders had to be addressed. This created a financial free for all, and the results were a windfall for some and merely a good deal for the rest. The merger, which occurred on December 22, 1914, and resulted in the (second) New York Central Railroad,

The 20th Century Limited — Eighteen Hour Train between New York and Chicago

TWO BELTS FOR THE CENTRAL

Two beltline-type railroads came into the New York Central fold early in the twentieth century: the Indiana Harbor Belt and the so-called Kankakee Belt. The IHB was formed in 1907 (although its infrastructure had been in place since the 1890s under the name East Chicago Belt Railroad) and was jointly owned by Michigan Central and Lake Shore & Michigan Southern. It served as a belt line linking the main MC and LS&MS facilities on Chicago's south side with various western connections on Chicago's southwest and west side. In 1911 ownership was split between NYC, Chicago & North Western, and Milwaukee Road. As of 1999, the IHB remained independent, though jointly owned by Conrail and Soo Line (Canadian Pacific), and continued to be an important transfer railroad for Chicagoland rail operations.

The Kankakee Belt was the successor to the Indiana, Illinois & Iowa—the "Three I"—launched in the 1880s as a Chicago bypass route. Upon completion in 1906, the 194-mile route stretched from South Bend, Indiana, west to Ladd in north-central Illinois by way of North Judson, Indiana, and

Indiana Harbor Belt switchers line up for duty at Blue Island yard on Chicago's South Side in 1958. *Richard J. Solomon*

Kankakee and Streator, Illinois. NYC took the line into its fold officially in 1914 and used it for traffic destined to and from western connections, notably the Santa Fe at Streator, the Rock Island at De Pue, Illinois, and the Burlington at Zearing, Illinois. The east end of the line offered connections as well, to the Monon, Nickel Plate, Chesapeake & Ohio, and Baltimore & Ohio, among others. As of 1999, NYC successor Conrail still used a portion of the line for Chicago bypass traffic, but the east end had been mostly abandoned.

left such an acrid taste in the mouths of management that the remaining affiliate roads—notably Big Four, Michigan Central, and the B&A—were left as long-term renewable leases unless the bondholders were friends or family.

NYC's Nickel Plate stock was sold to Cleveland's Van Sweringen brothers in 1915 as Smith divested the Central of the line at the urging of the U.S. Attorney General, for $8.5 million. Seemingly a bargain price, the move was the first in a series of events that foresaw the motives of land speculators, oil men, and stock manipulators all working in concert—as shareholders with the management of the line—to further their own goals at the expense of the railroad.

WORLD WAR I AND THE NYC

During World War I, Smith took a leave of absence from his presidency to serve as a regional chief for the United States Railroad Administration (USRA), formed to operate most of the nation's railroads during the war. For a year, William K. Vanderbilt Jr. served as Central's president, stepping down upon Smith's return. All was not well at the Central when armistice came in 1918, however. The war had strained the physical plant and stretched thin the railroad's finances. New rolling stock and locomotives were purchased to handle the massive wartime traffic, but the Interstate Commerce Commission had prohibited rate increases to cover the costs. In

SELKIRK YARD AND THE CASTLETON CUTOFF

A particularly notable engineering project of the twentieth century was the opening of Selkirk Yard and its associated Castleton Cutoff south of Albany. Central's Hudson Division had shared a crossing over the Hudson River at Albany opposite Rensselaer with the Boston & Albany since that road's inception. Two parallel drawbridges, one for freight trains and one for passenger, crossed the river, west of which all traffic was funneled into the Mohawk Division. The climb out of Albany up West Albany hill to West Albany Yard—Central's principal freight facility in the Capital Cities area—required pusher engines on most freights, which made for a second bottleneck.

The Castleton Cutoff relieved the congestion. The east end of the Cutoff connected with the B&A main line at Niverville. West from Niverville, the Cutoff crossed the Hudson on a gargantuan, mile-long bridge north of Schodack Landing. Named in honor of Central president Alfred Smith—who was largely responsible for the Castleton Cutoff project but died before construction began—the new Smith Bridge was designed to accommodate four tracks, but never carried more than two. It was one of the most imposing structures on the New York Central and still ranks among the largest railroad bridges east of the Mississippi River.

Once across the river, the Cutoff intersected the West Shore's Albany branch and ended at the new Selkirk Yard, which lay more or less parallel to the West Shore main line, at this point angling southeast–northwest. Hudson Division freights could reach the Cutoff on a new connection that involved a gentle, circling climb out of the Hudson River Valley floor north of Stuyvesant. Freights off the West Shore that stopped at Selkirk entered by way of the Albany branch. The west end of Selkirk Yard fed into the West Shore main line which bypassed Albany proper. Freights westbound out of Selkirk used the West Shore to a connection at Rotterdam Junction where they could continue straight along the West Shore or branch onto a connection to the NYC&HR main at Hoffmans.

The $25 million cutoff, opened in 1924, greatly eased operations by separating freight and passenger trains in the Albany area, shortening the freight route, and eliminating the need for westbound Boston & Albany freights to descend into the Hudson River Valley and then climb the 1.63 grade up West Albany Hill—the steepest mainline grade between New York City and Chicago. It also provided Hudson Line freights an alternate route through Albany, eliminating the need for westbound traffic out of New York City to ascend West Albany Hill as well.

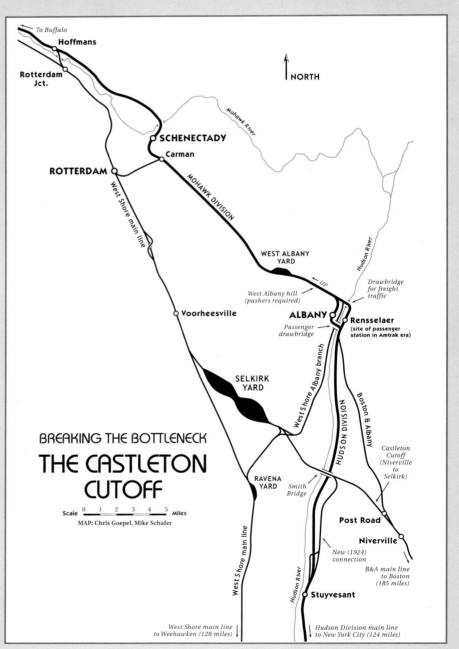

BREAKING THE BOTTLENECK
THE CASTLETON CUTOFF

MAP: Chris Goepel, Mike Schafer

1916 the work day was legally capped at eight hours for every worker in America, and once again the ICC refused the railroad in its request to raise freight and passenger rates to cover the resulting increase in expenses. By the time the United States entered the war in 1917, the Central had become a victim of deferred maintenance and freight-car shortages. The war only made things worse, and by 1920 over a billion dollars had to be spent to refurbish the New York Central System.

Shortly after the war ended, William K. Vanderbilt Sr. died at age 70. He had seen the Central go from being the exclusive province of his family to a vast corporation run by blocks of shareholders. Principal control during the early years of the twentieth century, despite the Vanderbilts' large holdings, had been the Rockefeller-Stillman-Morgan interests, three parties who had many interests in the line other than seeing it show a profit.

DEPRESSION AND ANOTHER WAR

The Great Depression that began with the stockmarket "Crash of '29" was foisted upon the Central with the same poor timing that was its trademark with all Eastern railroads. The massive renovation costs of the 1920s resulting from heavy wartime traffic had left NYC with a $670 million debt. Revenues in 1932 were at $293 million, and the railroad's stock price reflected the change in its operating ratio. Stocks fell from $130 per share in 1931 to $10 in 1932—the first year that the railroad didn't pay a dividend. Despite that, the Central didn't go bankrupt—but it had become a sorry shadow of its once mighty self. By 1939 the bulk of the railroad's locomotives and passenger cars were over 20 years old, the bright exception being new streamlined equipment introduced in 1938 on the *20th Century Limited* and its classy companion train, the *Commodore Vanderbilt*.

The outbreak of World War II was a boon to the railroad, as wartime business swelled traffic to capacity, allowing the railroad to shrink its long-term debt. Still, frugality was the order of the day; the per-share price rose to $35 by war's end in 1945. During World War II, American railroads remained independent of

The Depression ate into discretionary passenger travel, and passenger revenues fell drastically early in the 1930s. This view of the *Cleveland–St. Louis Special* westbound on the Big Four at Marion, Ohio, in 1933 illustrates the plight. Mail and express business appears to be brisk, but a smoker, single coach, and single sleeper are more than adequate to handle passenger loadings. *H. W. Pontin, Herbert H. Harwood collection*

Central's Ingenious Timesaver: The Water Pan

A spray of water from beneath the tender of Mohawk 3130 indicates this tank train is taking water on the fly from the track pans at Palmyra, New York, during the World War II era. *NYC, Tim Doherty collection*

New York Central was one of a few American railroads that employed water pans for replenishing locomotive tenders with water at speed. Maintaining proper water level in a locomotive's boiler was crucial to the efficient and safe operation of a steam locomotive. An overfilled boiler would not function properly, while an underfilled boiler was potentially explosive. Along with coal, water was stored in the tender that trailed behind the engine. To fill the tenders with water, railroads maintained water tanks and "plugs" (water dispensing stands) at strategic locations along the line. On most railroads, trains stopped to fill the tender at regular intervals, a slow but necessary process that necessarily lengthened train schedules. On the New York Central, speed and efficiency were

paramount concerns. To speed up operations and eliminate the need for time-wasting water stops, the railroad established a network of track pans along its famed Water Level Route.

A standard ratio for figuring water-to-coal consumption was 1,000 gallons per every 1.4 tons, and most railroads would balance the storage of these materials in tenders accordingly. An additional benefit to tracks pans was that locomotive tenders could carry proportionally more coal because they did not need to allocate as much space for water storage, thus minimizing fuel stops.

Central typically located track pans on level, tangent track. Pans were 19 inches wide, 8 inches deep, and placed midway between the rails, just

below rail level. The pans were of varied length, usually between 1,400 and 2,500 feet. Water tanks and pump houses were located adjacent to the main line at pan locations. In addition stationary steam plants were built to keep water free of ice in cold weather. A steam line injected live steam directly into the pans to keep water from freezing.

Special signals marked the beginning and ending of pans. Locomotives designed for taking water while moving ("on the fly") were equipped with telescopic water scoops attached to the tender and remotely controlled from the cab using an air-pressure cylinder. A train would typically slow to about 40 mph, and the crew would lower the scoop. Some late-era locomotives were equipped with high-speed water scoops that permitted scooping as fast as 75 miles per hour. For obvious reasons it was extremely important that the scoop was retracted before reaching the end of the pan. The scooping procedure was very messy, and a great quantity of water was splashed out of the pan as the locomotive took on water. For this reason, water recovery pans were typically located on both sides of the main tracks.

Working from east to west on its main New York—Chicago main line, NYC had pans at Clinton Point and Tivoli, New York, along the Hudson; at Schenectady, Yosts, Rome, Seneca River, Palmyra, Churchville, and Wende between Albany and Buffalo; at Silver Creek and Westfield, New York; Springfield, Pennsylvania; Painesville, Huron, and Stryker, Ohio; Corunna, Grismore, Lydick, and Chesterton, Indiana, between Buffalo and Chicago. When the railroad retired its steam, the track pans were removed and today there is virtually no physical evidence of these important time-saving devices.

the shackles of USRA-type control that had plagued them during World War I, and many historians feel that it was their finest hour. New York Central, like other roads, demonstrated Herculean effort at moving troops and war essentials—no small thanks to the renovations that Central had undertaken following World War I.

Gustav Meltzman took over as NYC president in 1944 after Frederick E. Williamson resigned due to poor health. Also that year, William K. Vanderbilt Jr. died, leaving his son Harold to carry on the family tradition of railroad management in the boardroom and on the executive committee.

As the winds of war faded, a wave of optimism swept across the nation, influencing Americans as individuals and corporations alike, including the nation's railroads. Initially, most railroads—and the NYC was certainly one of them—shared in this optimism, only to find that it veiled a bad hand of cards. American railroads had fought and won the biggest conflagration in world history, but they now faced an entirely new battle that focused on the railroad industry itself. And Central was in the thick of it.

In the summer of 1936 a local freight adds to the bustle of downtown Syracuse as its lopes through the business district. Trains were restricted to 15 mph on the Washington Street trackage, which crossed some 20 north-south streets. In September 1936, such scenes as this vanished when the new elevated bypass was opened. *Cal's Classics*

The year 1936 also saw Central's entry into streamlining with the debut of the *Mercury* between Cleveland and Detroit. *Mike Schafer collection*

Shrouded in the mists of time, an *Empire Service* corridor train lays over at the old Albany Union Station in 1968. Toward the end, NYC had all but given up on the long-distance passenger train, focusing instead on short-haul corridor-style operation—the prime route being New York–Albany–Buffalo. It was a half-hearted attempt, but not off the mark by any means and in some ways served as a foundation for today's successful high-speed Empire Corridor services offered by Amtrak. *Mike Schafer*

NEW YORK CENTRAL IN TWILIGHT

The Post-World War II Era:
Veiled Prosperity and Decline

With World War II behind, the nation stood poised on a new era of prosperity and growth—and radical changes to the way Americans approached life and carried out work. As a whole, U.S. railroads initially joined in this new momentum, but quickly fell behind. Despite the critical role that the railroads had played in World War II victory, the federal government soon turned its back on the railroad industry to embrace, more than ever, highway and air transport and foster massive improvements to the infrastructures of both.

The railroads were on their own, however, when it came to rebuilding themselves after the war, and they had to do so under a stranglehold of regulations that had been imposed on them since before the turn of the century. For example, railroads could not adjust tariffs and freight rates in accordance to fast-moving marketplace changes; approval had to be forthcoming from the monolithic Interstate Commerce Commission, an unwieldy procedure that could take months—if changes were approved at all. Such stiff regulatory practices were largely the result of the questionable behavior of railroad management during the railroads' stunning rise to power in the late 1800s, but even with those colorful years far behind, railroads remained chained.

Postwar highway and air-transport development proved a particularly nasty blow to railroads. On the New York Central, the Chicago–New York main line was under siege. A bustling postwar economy allowed more Americans to purchase automobiles, perhaps the ultimate symbol of freedom. As 1950 approached, Central embarked on a massive program to dieselize and re-equip its passenger trains with new cars, but the project only briefly delayed the inevitable mass flee to highways and new emerging airline systems. The motor-truck industry took its toll as well, as shippers found the benefits of truckload and door-to-door LTL (less-than-truckload) service, all accomplished in less time than it took to move freight by rail—and at competitive prices.

Costs began to escalate as railroad workers demanded more pay and less time on the job. Dieselization was a major factor in cost reduction for railroads everywhere, but it required massive capital investment. Although several other railroads had begun dieselization in earnest prior to World War II, Central did not embark upon a comprehensive dieselization program until the late 1940s. It would take nearly a decade to complete, during which time the Central had to address declining freight and passenger revenues.

Under NYC President Gustave Metzman, passenger equipment upgrade projects and dieselization were launched. Metzman was succeeded early in the 1950s by William R. White, who at the time of this appointment was president of the Delaware, Lackawanna & Western, in which NYC had a vested interest. (As such, NYC stipulated that the Lackawanna's New York [Hoboken]–Buffalo trains could not offer faster schedules than NYC trains which took the longer route between the two cities via Albany. Lackawanna trains

After World War II, the nemesis of the New York Central was not necessarily the Pennsylvania Railroad, nor any other railroad for that matter. It was the highway, in the form of the trucking company and private automobile. On a bright June afternoon in 1959, a northbound T-motor races the competition on the Bronx River Parkway at Williams Bridge, New York, on the Harlem Line. *Richard J. Solomon*

could have easily bettered NYC schedules.)

White was a railroad man from the old school, rising through the ranks of the Erie Railroad before going on to management positions at the Virginian Railway and the Lackawanna. White toured the Central extensively to assess the railroad's problem areas and went to great lengths to improve the manner in which NYC addressed the needs of shippers, employees, and on-line communities. A consulting firm was hired to analyze the top end of the company and make recommendations on how management could streamline its decision-making process.

By 1953, White's work began to pay off. Central's management, always top heavy with vice presidents, had been cut; dieselization continued, property taxes were reduced, and new train schedules were implemented that improved car utilization. Repairs to trackage and rolling stock were having an positive effect as freight began moving more smoothly over the line once more. Passenger operations were trimmed, as there had been as much as a 70 percent decrease in ridership on many runs

compared to previous years—certainly due to the huge inroads that had been made by automobiles and airlines.

In June 1953 the ICC issued a decision regarding the division of line-haul revenue between connecting railroads. Formerly the division was tilted in favor of Western railroads where line-haul distances were much greater overall, but the new decision split the revenue evenly and the NYC benefited to the tune of $8 million a year in additional revenue. But ill winds continued to blow, this time in the form of Robert R. Young.

Young and his band of corporate raiders had been eyeing the NYC for a long time. In a style reminiscent of Commodore Vanderbilt, Young had accumulated 10 per cent of Central's stock and ran a harsh publicity campaign in the newspapers bemoaning the performance of the White administration. In January 1954 a wicked proxy battle ensued, fueled by the railroad's poor showing during the nationwide business slowdown in late 1953 and the widely held notion that White and company were ruining the railroad. Young's relentless

Double-headed B&A Berkshires led by Class A-1c No. 1448 slug it out on the climb to Charlton, Massachusetts, with an eastbound freight at Warren in 1948. *R. E. Tobey, collection of Herbert H. Harwood Jr.*

For much of the twentieth century, Central offered passenger service to nearly all corners of its system. But by the end of the 1950s, service was severely curtailed or eliminated altogether on many lines. Once a popular tourist route with through sleeping-car service out of New York and Chicago, the Adirondack line was one of many to feel the pinch of auto competition. In this 1958 view at Thendara (Old Forge), New York, the day train between Lake Placid and Utica is down to a single coach. *Mike Schafer collection*

campaign put him on TV and radio, in magazines, and in newspaper ads. In June 1954 he won his fight to control the Central, wiping out the last of the Vanderbilt stockholders. White resigned, and Young brought in Alfred E. Perlman from the Denver & Rio Grande Railroad to serve as NYC's president.

From the start, Perlman's ideas ran contrary to incumbent management's notions of what constituted Central's problems. After touring the railroad with his staff, Perlman concluded that the NYC wasn't getting the utilization out its new diesel electric locomotives that it should, that the line's yards needed complete rebuilding, and that the organizational setup that the railroad had just laboriously implemented was all wrong. As the country's economy gathered speed, the earnings of the railroad, not surprisingly, improved. Young was quick to take credit for the improvement in the bottom line.

The traffic rebound had its backlashes, though, primarily a consistent shortage of motive power. As the Central's once mighty fleet of steam locomotives wore out, they were scrapped rather than repaired, as the road's back shops had been closed as an economy measure. New diesel-electric locomotives had been ordered to replace them, but one of Perlman's first edicts in 1954 was to cut new diesel

A pair of seven-year-old Alco freight cab units wheel along former West Shore trackage near Chili Junction (Rochester), New York, on June 30, 1956. By this time, NYC president Al Perlman was convinced that the railroad was not fully utilizing its existing diesel fleet and cut orders for new diesels. The plan would soon backfire. *John Dziobko*

orders in half, claiming that more mileage could be squeezed out of the existing diesel fleet. This logic was based on the Santa Fe's diesel utilization, and Perlman reasoned that whatever worked on the industry's golden-haired carrier would work on the Central. But, the Santa Fe and NYC were two different animals. Santa Fe's long freight and passenger runs—up to 2,000 miles at a crack—naturally made better use of diesels. Central's train operations consisted of much shorter runs overall, with locomotive utilization unavoidingly less efficient. By the time Perlman realized the flaw in his logic, nearly all the available new locomotive production had been allocated to other railroads deep in the throes of dieselization. By the end of 1955, service had slipped considerably, with trains sitting in yards waiting for available locomotives to haul them.

In 1954 the old guard, led by NYC operating vice president Karl A. Borntrager, proposed to establish TOFC (trailer-on-flatcar) or "piggyback" service, but Young and Perlman put the kibosh on the idea—only to reinvent it in 1957 after Borntrager retired. (One might speculate that this change of heart might have been prompted by rival Pennsylvania Railroad's success with its "TrucTrain" piggyback service, launched in 1954.)

In 1955 Perlman introduced a new management team, headed by K. L. Moriarity—another graduate of D&RGW. Young and Perlman were convinced that they were on a prudent

Railroading's classic steam-to-diesel transition period is embodied in this 1953 scene at Rensselaer, New York, as Hudson 5415 tromps into town from Troy, New York, in late afternoon with the *Laurentian* from Montreal. Jointly operated with Delaware & Hudson, the *Laurentian* and other New York–Montreal runs were handled by NYC between Grand Central and Troy; later, Albany. *NYC, Jim Boyd collection*

MOTIVE-POWER POOLING

To eliminate costly switching and transfer operations at interchange points, railroads sometimes blocked entire trains for interchange with connecting railroads. Ideally, the whole train should be able to run through from one railroad to another, including locomotives, but this was not economically and operationally viable during the steam era, so only the cars themselves were forwarded on through. Steam locomotives required significant mechanical attention every hundred miles or so, and at a division point where the interchange was likely to be made, the locomotive usually had to be removed from the train anyway for servicing.

Even if that wasn't the case, there were other barriers that prevented steam locomotives from operating through to other roads. Steam-locomotive design and technology tended to vary widely from railroad to railroad, with locomotives sharing few, if any, interchangeable parts with other locomotives even on the home railroad, much less a connecting railroad. Regardless of the skills of one railroad's mechanical department, they were hardly in a position to repair a locomotive of another carrier without a stock of parts from the home road, and this simply was not economical.

Diesel-electric locomotive technology changed all that. By the end of the 1950s, railroads had learned that diesels could run continuously for hundreds, even thousands of miles without undue mechanical attention, stopping only for fuel. Diesels were mass-produced with interchangeable parts; roundhouse stockrooms on neighboring railroads now brimmed with the repair parts that would work on a New York Central Electro-Motive F-series freight diesel just as well as it would a Burlington Route F-series unit. Now both the motive power and the train could operated right through congested terminals with minimal delay.

The railroads kept accounts of loco-

In the mid-1960s, New York Central and Rock Island jointly operated a through freight train between Elkhart, Indiana, and Silvis (Rock Island), Illinois. Known as the *Gemini* (in honor of ongoing space-travel developments of the era), the train ran on the Kankakee Belt from South Bend to De Pue, Illinois, thence west on the Rock Island. Motive power was pooled, as shown in this scene of the westbound *Gemini* at Wyanet, Illinois, in 1965. *Mike Schafer*

motive mileages on foreign roads, and any imbalances were reconciled by agreement, with either a fixed cost-per-mile charge or loaner diesel locomotives to run off the owed mileage. The whole process became known as motive-power "pooling." NYC was an early and eager participant in motive-power pools and run-through trains. The table below shows most of the pooling arrangements in which the Central participated.

Foreign locomotives from CB&Q, MP, B&M and others could be regularly see on these runs, and many other parts of the system running off excess mileage. Many of these pooling arrangements persisted and grew following the Penn Central merger.— *James Mischke*

Connecting Road	End Terminals and Routing
Atchison Topeka & Santa Fe	Elkhart, Indiana–Argentine, Kansas, via Chicago
Boston & Maine	Cleveland–New England via Mechanicville, N.Y.
Chicago Burlington & Quincy	Elkhart–Omaha, Nebraska, via Chicago
Chicago, Rock Island & Pacific	Elkhart–Silvis, Illinois, via the Kankakee Belt
Missouri Pacific	Cleveland, Ohio–Little Rock, Arkansas, via St. Louis
Missouri Pacific	Cleveland–Kansas City, Missouri, via St. Louis
St. Louis-Southwestern (Cotton Belt)	Cleveland–Pine Bluff, Arkansas, via St. Louis

course and that the Central would once again make $100 million dollars a year, just like it had in 1929. But in 1929, passenger service was still turning a profit; now, it was losing $38 million yearly. Young ballyhooed that his planned "Train-X" —a streamliner of radical (read, unproven) technology that had yet to see the light of day—would reverse this loss. When Train-X was unveiled, it promptly crashed and burned—figuratively—and Young quietly gave up his idea as critics of the railroad's handling of passenger service became more vocal.

The one bright star during this twilight period for Central was the Flexi-Van, a pioneering intermodal concept that combined TOFC's best attributes with that of containerization, still very much in infancy. (See chapter 9 for a more detailed explanation of the Flexi-Van.) Though Flexi-Van was considered a success, Central was still reeling from the loss of traffic to trucking lines using their new set of "tracks," the New York State Thruway, Ohio Turnpike, and Indiana Toll Road, all paralleling Central's New York–Chicago main line. Boat traffic on the improved St. Lawrence Seaway also gnawed into NYC's Great Lakes–Eastern Seaboard traffic.

Perlman's contention was that the federal government should assist the NYC through these lean times and subsidize the remaining passenger traffic. After testifying at a Congressional hearing on the subject of NYC's plight and realizing that no help was forthcoming (in those years, federal and state governments were less inclined toward subsidies), Young and Perlman addressed the inevitable: merge or sink. Young began talking with B&O and C&O about merging, only to be turned down. (Hindsight now suggests that either might have enjoyed a successful union with NYC.) During this same period, the Pennsylvania Railroad faced similar financial woes and merger rebuffs. Major differences notwithstanding, NYC and PRR turned to each other.

Although the idea of merging two railroads that closely duplicated each other's systems is now known as a recipe for disaster, PRR Chairman James Symes and Central's Young had several meetings during 1957. The seriousness of Central's condition was underscored by an unexpected event that stunned industry officials and to this day is steeped in mystery: In January 1958, Young committed suicide. Negotiations between

A 1954 view of the Harlem River swing bridge and a Grand Central-bound NYC train reveals a major-league upgrade project under way. Under construction at left is the new Harlem River lift bridge which will provide greater clearances for marine traffic. In the distance and partially obscured by the new bridge is the 138th Street station for the Bronx. *John Dziobko*

L-3a Mohawk 3010 charges off the Wabash River bridge on the Big Four main line at Terre Haute, Indiana, with an eastbound freight in May 1956. A sunny day it may be, but it's twilight for the steam era of New York Central. *Lou Marre collection*

the two adversaries stalled, but Perlman stepped in to revive them. Perlman and Symes had a strong dislike for one another, but by 1961 they were able to craft an agreement. In 1963 Symes retired and was replaced with Stuart Saunders, who carried on the tradition of not getting along with Perlman. It took until 1966 for the Interstate Commerce Commission to approve the merger of the two giants. The new railroad, Penn Central Transportation Company, would have Saunders as its chairman of the board and Perlman as its president—a combination as lethal as the two railroads themselves. The merger was consummated on February 1, 1968 (perhaps significantly, less than two months after the abrupt and controversial demise of the *20th Century Limited*) and the once-mighty New York Central System vanished into history.

One NYC innovation that was in part ahead of its time was the Flexi-Van. One of the pioneering cars is shown fully loaded at Dayton, Ohio, in 1965. The Flexi-Van system could be considered a precursor of the type of container format widely found on today's railroads. On the NYC, Flexis could be found on freight as well as passenger trains. *Lou Marre collection*

Central's *Ohio Xplorer* at Cincinnati Union Terminal in 1956 portended a modern new era for passenger trains. The forecast was actually half right, for although the little Talgo-style train was a failure for NYC, its modern-day descendants were drawing rave reviews on Amtrak in 1999. *Lou Marre collection*

The Penn Central merger has happened, but for all the world this scene at Cleveland Union Terminal—a centerpiece building for downtown Cleveland—still looks like the New York Central. Westbound nameless train 63, a remnant of the old New York–Chicago *Iroquois*, is just getting under way for its daylight trek across Ohio and Indiana. *Allan H. Roberts*

The splendor of
Grand Central
Terminal survives
85 years after its
completion in
1913. *Brian
Solomon*

5

GRAND CENTRAL AND THE NEW YORK ELECTRIFICATION

A Gift to New Yorkers and a Monument to the New York Central

Grand Central Terminal is without doubt the most famous railroad station in the world. Its very name has become synonymous with "busy," and certainly GCT is the nation's largest and for many years was the busiest railroad station. However, Grand Central is far more than mere depot. Its vast size and extraordinary splendor symbolized New York Central's enormous power, and the station has come to epitomize the golden age of American railroads in the early twentieth century.

Grand Central Terminal was the gateway to America's largest city during the era when American railroads were among the most powerful corporations in the world. Despite the American railroads' loss of supremacy, their slow decline as passenger carriers, and the demise of the NYC, Grand Central remains a vital part of the city it was designed to serve. It is the foremost example of Beaux Arts architecture in America and one of the most famous buildings in New York City. When Grand Central was rededicated in October 1998, the station made national news, and today appears as glamorous as it did when it originally opened in 1913.

The site of the first Grand Central dates from the late 1860s when Commodore Vanderbilt began consolidating the main passenger facilities of his Hudson River Railroad and the New York & Harlem at 42nd Street in Manhattan; the New York & New Haven would become a tenant. (The distinctly northerly location of this combined facility stemmed from an 1859 law precluding the use of steam locomotives south of 42nd Street. The old NY&H terminal had been at 27th, near what is today Madison Square Garden.) Opened in late 1871, Vanderbilt's new terminal took the name Grand Central Depot as a result of this great terminal consolidation. The facility—technically built by the NY&H—included an enormous balloon train shed erected in the image of London's pioneering St. Pancras iron shed dating from 1867. Grand Central's vast shed was 600 feet long, 200 feet wide, 100 feet tall at its apex, and spanned 12 tracks. Alas, depot design and operations were poorly planned, and the chaotic facility soon became known as "Grand Swindle Depot".

The unusually rapid growth of New York City in the post-Civil War period had an enormous influence on railroad operations and facilities. Commuter traffic, nearly non-existent before the war, grew rapidly as New York expanded and in a short time suburban passengers greatly outnumbered long-distance travelers. By the mid-1870s the exceptionally high train frequency on the Park Avenue line that lead to Grand Central forced the railroad to build a costly grade separation. Between the throat of Grand Central at 45th Street and 98th Street the railroad was depressed in cuts and tunnels, while beyond 98th, through Harlem, the tracks rode on an elevated stone viaduct.

In the 1880s traffic into Grand Central exceeded the capacity of the station, and in

The original Grand Central, opened in 1871, is shown following its turn-of-the-century revamp in which the track capacity was increased and the architecture updated. Today's Grand Central sits on the same site on 42nd Street. *Mike Schafer collection*

1885 and 1886 the railroad was compelled to construct a seven-track addition and auxiliary train shed. In addition, the NYC&HR built a large passenger-car yard at Mott Haven (near today's Yankee Stadium) in the Bronx to relieve congestion at smaller facilities near Grand Central. In 1898 the railroad embarked an a large-scale remodeling of its New York terminal to accommodate more tracks and greater passenger volumes. Following this rebuilding, the terminal was known for a short time as Grand Central Station, a name that stuck in the minds of most travelers and is still often used today when referring to the present structure. (Technically, Grand Central Station now refers to the postal station within Grand Central Terminal.) Despite this expansion, the station was still straining from capacity problems, and it was obvious that an entirely new station was needed. In 1900 Grand Central was already handling more than three times the number of trains it had in 1871, and the rate of growth was still rising.

PLANNING A NEW GRAND CENTRAL AND ELECTRIFICATION

Grand Central Station was accommodating roughly 500 scheduled trains daily at the turn of the century in addition to dozens of light engine moves and equipment positioning runs. Outside of raw congestion, one of the most serious problems was the smoke produced by hundreds of steam locomotives congregating at the station. A more serious problem was the build-up of smoke in the tunnels along Park Avenue. At times the smoke was so severe it obscured signals, slowed operations, and increased the likelihood of collision.

William Wilgus, vice president and chief engineer of the NYC&HR, was among the most talented railroad engineers of his generation and the visionary genius behind the building and electrification of Grand Central. He considered electrification as a solution to Grand Central's smoke and capacity problems as early as 1899. Electrification would permit the construction of a below-ground, two-level train platform area. A disastrous accident in the Park Avenue tunnel on January 8, 1902, forced the issue. On that fateful morning, an inbound train overran a stop signal in one of the smoke-filled Park Avenue tunnels and crashed into the end of a fully loaded New Haven commuter train, killing 15 passengers. The press sensationalized the wreck, and public outcry encouraged the city to pass strict legislation that forced the railroad to eliminate steam-locomotive operation into Grand Central by July 1, 1908.

An Electric Traction Commission comprising many of the most respected authorities of the time—including Frank J. Sprague, one of the great electric-railway pioneers—was established to study electrification options. The Central decided to electrify Grand Central and, indeed, its whole Manhattan terminal district using a 660-volt DC third-rail system based on the success of Baltimore & Ohio's Howard Street Tunnel electrification and New York's rapid transit system, both of which employed third-rail distribution. NYC's system was slightly different in that it employed a uniquely designed "under-running" third rail in which the top of the rail was covered with wood while the underside was left exposed for locomotive collector shoes that pressed upward. This design was less likely to be affected by snow and ice and potentially safer for people and animals who strayed onto the tracks.

The electrification process began in 1903. Electric service into Grand Central proper preceded completion of the new terminal building (construction of which had also commenced in 1903) and was inaugurated on September 20, 1906, although steam locomotives continued to serve the station on a limited basis a while longer. At this time, electrification extended only as far north as High Bridge, seven miles out of Grand Central; electrification on the Harlem Line opened as far as Wakefield, 13 miles from Grand Central, in 1907. In 1910 electrification was extended north from Wakefield 11 miles to North White Plains and in 1913 to Croton, 33 miles north of Grand Central on the Hudson Line.

In 1926 electrification was extended up a short branch of the Putnam Division to Getty Square. Also during the late 1920s and until 1931, NYC electrified its primary New York terminal area freight routes as part of a large-scale freight-service improvement plan, including the West Side Freight Line in Manhattan and the Port Morris branch in the South Bronx. Nearly 70 route-miles had been electrified by the end of 1931.

In addition to the electric locomotives that were used to haul trains over the electrified routes (chapter 8), the Central employed self-propelled electric M.U. (multiple-unit) passenger cars expressly for local train service. M.U. cars featured axle-mounted traction motors which drew current from the third rail; the cars were operated by crews from car-end control cabs.

Central's freight electrification was relatively short-lived, surviving less than three decades. By the mid-1950s the railroad had completely dieselized its steam operations in the New York area and saw little need to maintain the freight electrification, and it was thus discontinued.

GRAND CENTRAL TERMINAL

Work on the new $43 million Grand Central Terminal took nearly a decade to complete. William H. Newman would resign as NYC president in 1909 so he could devote all his time to the completion of the terminal, such was the size of this undertaking.

Construction was complicated and delayed by the need to keep ad hoc passenger facilities open for the full daily schedule of 400 trains during the duration of construction. The initial Grand Central design was awarded to Minnesota's Charles Reed and Allen H. Stem, noted architects responsible for numerous railroad station designs. Soon after Reed & Stem drew up early plans for the new terminal building, Warren & Wetmore was hired to assist. Whitney Warren, the firm's principal architect (and

Initially, electrification on the Hudson Line extended only as far as High Bridge in the Bronx. In this 1911 view, the *20th Century Limited* has just exchanged its steam locomotive for a stout little S-motor for the remainder of the trip to GCT. *Cal's Classics*

Right on time at 12:15 p.m., an elderly T-motor hums into the 125th Street station in Manhattan with train No. 1034 from Brewster on Nov. 8, 1958. *Richard J. Solomon*

a cousin to the Vanderbilts), was accomplished in his trade, having studied at the École des Beaux Arts in Paris and later working for McKim, Mead & White, the prestigious New York firm responsible for the design of Pennsylvania Station that would open in 1910. Although Charles Reed and Whitney Warren are usually credited as the principle architects of the depot building, the design specifics are embroiled in controversy.

Reed worked with Wilgus to provide the basis of Grand Central's revolutionary design incorporating the pioneering use of a two-level station with reverse loops, an exceptional pedestrian traffic flow pattern using gently sloping ramps rather than stairs, and the extension of Park Avenue around the station using what Reed described as "exterior circumferential elevated driveways." Wetmore is responsible for Grand Central's monumental presence, exquisite refinement, and Beaux Arts embellishment that has made the station the most impressive railroad facility in the world. There were considerable visionary differences between Reed and Wetmore that resulted in numerous changes in Grand Central's plan before the station was completed. Following Charles Reed's death in 1911, two years prior to the completion of Grand Central, Warren & Wetmore assumed full control of the project and finished the great station.

Grand Central Terminal fulfilled the monumental visions of its builders. It is an awe-inspiring structure that conveys the imperial presence of the New York Central Railroad of the early twentieth century. The main concourse—275 feet long and 120 feet wide—is a vast space that dwarfs the individual and can accommodate tens of thousands of daily pedestrians. Rising 125 feet above the floor is a great celestial ceiling depicting the Zodiac in the Mediterranean sky. The interior stone is a veneer of marble and simulated Caen stone (true Caen stone is quarried in Normandy). Grand Central's exterior is comprised of Bedford (Indiana) limestone and Stony Creek granite. Three enormous windows, each 33 feet wide and 60 feet tall, allow light into the station from its primary façade facing Park Avenue. Punctuating this great façade is an enormous sculpture and clock resting atop the building. This classically inspired work features the mythical Roman gods and goddess Mercury, Minerva, and Hercules. Mercury stands 29 feet tall, and the great clock face, perpetually reminding passengers and passers by of the time, is 13 feet in diameter.

The celestial ceiling is the work of prominent French painter Paul Helleu. The painting encompasses the whole ceiling and embodies 2,500 stars, 50 of which are illuminated (formerly with tiny bulbs and currently with fiber optics) for effect. The

Grand Central Terminal, New York.

breathtaking celestial art has a controversial side: except for the constellation of Orion, the entire sky is a mirror image of that seen in the Mediterranean. Over the years there has been much criticism over this perceived flaw and speculation as to why it was painted this way.

The station was designed to separate suburban passengers from long-distance travelers. In its heyday, suburban trains would primarily use the lower level, keeping the upper level free for intercity trains. Grand Central Terminal featured a full variety of services for railroad passengers and incorporated within the station were a potpourri of businesses making the station a precursor to the fully enclosed shopping mall. Numerous subterranean passageways connect Grand Central with nearby buildings and New York's comprehensive subway system.

From 96th Street south the mainline tracks leading to Grand Central were covered over and a new, wide Park Avenue was built above. Owned by NYC interests, the "air rights" above the covered right-of-way were leased—an arrangement that made the Grand Central project financially feasible. Today, these properties that line Park Avenue are among the highest in value anywhere in the world.

RUSH HOUR AT GRAND CENTRAL

The enormous growth in railroad ridership during the early twentieth century encouraged Grand Central's architects to anticipate tremendous future growth, and their designs reflected this. In 1902 the old Grand Central experienced a weekday average of 48,600 passengers, accommodating a total of nearly 15.6 million passengers during the year. In 1913 when the new Grand Central Terminal opened, the weekday average had jumped to 68,700 people, with a total of nearly 22 million people. By the mid-1920s these statistics had doubled, and in 1945 and 1946 as World War II wound down, Grand Central handled its largest crowds—more than 200,000 people daily for year-long totals exceeding 63 million. Yet the station's capacity was never strained beyond its designers' limits: 100 million yearly passengers! What the designers had failed to anticipate was the effect of the automobile on railroad transportation. By 1968 Grand Central's daily passenger count had receded to just 138,500 daily passengers for a yearly total of just over 44 million.

At its peak in the mid-1940s, Grand Central accommodated roughly 550 daily trains and employed more than 3,000 people to keep the station functioning. Although some tracks are assigned three-digit numbers, the station has just 48 platforms—still the most of any station in the United States. To keep traffic fluid, several subterranean control towers were built to operate switches and signals. Grand Central's two primary towers were among the largest in the United States Tower A featured 362 control levers while Tower B had a 400-lever plant, and as many as six signalmen were required to operate each tower during rush hours. The towers are now closed and Grand Central is dispatched remotely. Long-distance trains no longer use the famous station, but Grand Central remains one of America's busiest railroad terminals.

In the mid-1960s, the financially strapped Pennsylvania Railroad sold the air rights above its Pennsylvania Station south of Grand Central and demolished the massive structure which for decades had served as a worthy rival of Grand Central's grandeur. A similar fate loomed over Grand Central, but public outcry spearheaded by the late Jacqueline (Kennedy) Onassis resulted in a happy ending. Grand Central was declared a national historical landmark and, finally, during the 1990s, it underwent a massive renovation that restored Manhattan's jewel to its 1913 glory.

This 1998 view of the ticket area of the concourse graphically illustrates—aside from the splendid rehabilitation efforts—that Grand Central's reputation as a busy place remains unchallenged. *Brian Solomon*

Save for streamlined locomotives, modern steam on the New York Central presented a utilitarian face that was nonetheless impressive. Witness "elephant-eared" Mohawk (4-8-2) No. 3032 hurtling along with a westbund heavyweight Big Four passenger train at Dayton, Ohio, in the late 1950s. Once the smoke and dust had cleared, there was little doubt that an onlooker had gotten at least a brief lesson in the dynamics that could be unleashed by a combination of coal, fire, and water. As for those elephant-ear shrouds, they helped keep the steam and smoke out of the locomotive cab. *Alvin Schultze*

6

THE STEAM LOCOMOTIVE FLEET OF NEW YORK CENTRAL

From 4-4-0s to the Mighty Hudson

New York Central and its affiliates had one of the largest steam-locomotive fleets in the United States. In many respects, the bulk of Central's locomotive fleet reflected common trends in American motive-power development. For example, the railroad relied heavily on 4-4-0s ("American" type) until the development of larger, more powerful types. For freight service, it progressed from 4-4-0s to 2-8-0s (Consolidation), then embraced the 2-8-2 Mikado and later the 4-8-2 and briefly the 4-8-4. For its passenger service NYC embraced Atlantics (4-4-2), then the Pacific (4-6-2) in a typical pattern.

Yet, New York Central was an innovator. In the nineteenth century, the Central was noted for exceptionally refined locomotives, Central's famous 999 (see chapter 10 for a photo of 999 doing what it did best) being the most well-known example. During the twentieth century, NYC played a more prominent role in locomotive development and was closely involved with the development of the 2-8-4 Berkshire and 4-6-4 Hudson. New York Central's locomotives are considered by many authorities to be among the most efficient, exhibiting the highest level of refinement achieved in steam locomotive design: Central's steam was the best of the best.

NYC was among the last railroads to give up on steam power. It continued innovative steam research until after World War II, and its Pittsburgh & Lake Erie affiliate bought new steam locomotives as late as 1948 when most American lines were strictly buying diesels. Once dieselization began, Central quickly converted its eastern lines, and gradually worked westward. The Boston & Albany was fully dieselized by 1951; lines east of Buffalo were converted by 1953; and Central's last steam run occurred on May 2, 1957, at Cincinnati, Ohio. Unlike other lines, including rival Pennsylvania Railroad, that preserved examples of their steam fleet for posterity, NYC sent virtually its entire fleet to scrap. A few antiques, such as No. 999, are preserved, but there are no examples of modern New York Central locomotives, save lone Mohawk No. 3001 that miraculously escaped scrapping and is now displayed along Norfolk Southern's former Conrail, nee New York Central, main line at Elkhart, Indiana.

EARLY STEAM

New York Central's predecessors operated a variety of curious primitive machines in the formative years of railroading. Among these was Mohawk & Hudson's pioneering *De Witt Clinton*, an 0-4-0 built by the West Point Foundry. This distinctive-looking machine was designed by Adam Hall to meet the railroad's requirement for a locomotive that would haul 10 tons at 15 miles per hour on a grade of slightly less than one half percent. It is generally credited as the third locomotive manufactured by West Point Foundry and the first steam locomotive to operate in revenue service in New York State. It did not perform well and only operated for about a year. It was followed by an imported Stephenson locomotive named *Robert Fulton*, sometimes called the *John Bull* (not to be confused with the Camden & Amboy's import of the same name from the same period.) These locomotives were followed by the 4-2-0 *Experiment*, an engine designed by M&H's engineer, John B. Jervis, and built by the West Point Foundry. It was the first locomotive to feature a twin-axle swiveling lead truck (or "bogie"), a modification specifically designed to improve tracking. This locomotive influenced American-based locomotive development and led to the design of the first 4-4-0 "American" or "American Standard" type.

In the late 1830s and 1840s, New York Central's component lines employed a variety of 4-2-0s using Bury fireboxes featuring a prominent hemispherical dome used to achieve greater heating surface. These locomotives were constructed by a variety of builders including Baldwin, Rogers, and Norris, and like most early engines they did not feature trappings now associated with steam locomotives such as pilots, cabs, bells or headlights. These additions would come later.

The American Standard—the 4-4-0—was the predominant type used on most American railroads between 1850 and the turn of the century; Central and its affiliated lines were no exception, with several notable 4-4-0 designs. In the 1850s, Walter McQueen became the chief locomotive designer for the Schenectady Locomotive Works. He was noted for his exceptional locomotive designs and set a high standards for the industry. NYC, one of Schenectady's best customers, operated a great number of McQueen 4-4-0s. Another man that had a decisive influence on the building and development of NYC's 4-4-0s was William Buchanan, a talented engineer who began his railroad career with the Albany & Schenectady (successor company to the Mohawk & Hudson). He later worked for the Hudson River Railroad and ultimately Vanderbilt's New York Central & Hudson River where he served as the superintendent of motive power until just before the end of the nineteenth century. His locomotives were known for their exceptional performance and efficiency. To obtain better fuel efficiency, he

designed and patented the water-table firebox, which increased the heating area and coal combustion by partitioning the firebox using an enclosed table containing water tubes.

In the late 1880s and 1890s Buchanan refined the 4-4-0 into a powerful, speedy machine. His fast 4-4-0s used higher boiler pressure than typical American locomotives of the period, and featured tall driving wheels—between 70 and 84 inches. The most famous of these locomotives, although atypical, was NYC&HR No. 999, a locomotive often credited for setting the world speed record at 112.5 mph, an achievement whose authenticity has been questioned.

The 4-4-0 wheel arrangement had a long life on the NYC and some survived in branch-line service well into the 1930s. However most 4-4-0s were off the roster by 1910, having been replaced by larger, more powerful machines.

MIKADOS AND CONSOLIDATIONS

Central adopted the 2-8-2 Mikado type later than some railroads, but in a relatively short time came to operate the largest American fleet of Mikados. By the mid 1920s New York Central Lines had more than 1,200 Mikados in service, representing more than 10 percent of all Mikados built in the U.S. for domestic use. Mikados were employed systemwide in freight service, and many survived right to the very end of steam operations in 1957.

Baldwin developed the 2-8-2 in the 1890s as an export locomotive, and Baldwin made a significant sale of 2-8-2s to Japan about the time the Gilbert & Sullivan opera "The Mikado" (about imperial Japan) was enjoying great popularity in America. The locomotives became associated with the opera and the name stuck. The Mikado was developed for domestic use in 1903, and in 1904 Northern Pacific endorsed the type, placing the first large order for 2-8-2s. A significant advantage of the 2-8-2 over the earlier 2-8-0 was the addition of the trailing truck which permitted a substantially larger firebox grate resulting in greater boiler capacity and a significantly more-powerful locomotive.

While the 2-8-2 was gaining acceptance as the next generation of standard freight locomotive, NYC and its affiliate lines were taking delivery of hundreds of conventional G-5-class 2-8-0 Consolidations. Although these were reliable locomotives that represented highly

refined nineteenth century technology, they did not embrace modern technological developments and were largely inferior to modern 2-8-2s. By 1907, NYC had amassed a fleet of 595 G-5s.

By 1912 the railroad found it needed faster and more powerful freight locomotives, and the "superheated" Mikado was a substantially more capable locomotive than the saturated Consolidation. Yet, NYC was not anxious to retire its vast fleet of nearly new 2-8-0s and decided that rebuilding its G-5s into modern Mikados was the most cost-effective solution for satisfying its motive-power needs.

Some G-5s were upgraded to G-6 Consolidations, but 462 G-5s were rebuilt into H-5 Mikados. Rebuilding was performed by both Baldwin and Alco, and the work included new cylinders, pistons, piston rods, valves, valve gear, and the addition of steam superheaters and other modern innovations. The locomotives retained 63-inch wheels, which was accepted as the standard diameter for freight locomotives. The conversions proved highly successful: the rebuilt H-5s were significantly more powerful than G-5s. The success of the H-5 conversions led Central to purchase an additional 179 H-5s from Alco and Lima Locomotive Works—which had just entered the road locomotive business in 1914. Coincident with the rebuilding of the H-5, NYC ordered a fleet of heavier Mikados, Class H-7, for its western lines. In 1918 and 1919, Central acquired the largest fleet of United States Railroad Administration (USRA)-designed 2-8-2s, and classed them H-6 and H-9.

Lima, under the direction of William Woodard, was looking to revolutionize the locomotive industry and build a substantially more-efficient, more-powerful locomotives. In 1922 Lima worked with NYC in building an experimental super-Mikado prototype, No. 8000, Class H-10—an improvement upon Central's successful H-7 design. Although this new locomotive was only nominally heavier than the H-7, it produced 63,500 pounds tractive effort—7.6 percent greater than the H-7—and with the addition of a trailing truck booster engine it produced 26.3 percent more tractive effort when starting from a dead stop. The H-10 employed 63-inch drivers and operated at a boiler pressure of 200 psi. Number 8000 featured an enlarged firebox and significantly more grate area, an Elesco feedwater heater (used to feed pre-warmed water into the boiler), slightly larger cylinders (28 x 30 inches as opposed to 27 x 30 on the H-7), and Baker valve gear. It also used lightweight main and side rods constructed of modern alloy steel. Lighter reciprocating parts resulted in 50 percent less damage from pounding actions—known as dynamic augment—a great improvement over earlier designs. Central was extremely impressed by Lima's H-10 and ordered an additional 300 locomotives. A total of 115 were delivered by Lima, the remainder by Alco, NYC's primary locomotive supplier.

BERKSHIRES

Research and development of the H-10 was a step toward the designing of one of the most significant locomotive types in the twentieth century: Lima's 2-8-4 Berkshire, a locomotive that influenced most subsequent American steam-locomotive designs. Based on the principle that abundant steam in conjunction with other efficiency improvements would allow a locomotive to develop significantly greater

Early in the twentieth century, freight locomotives on the Lake Shore & Michigan Southern were predominately 2-8-0s; the railroad owned hundreds of them. The 912 was built at the turn of the century by Brooks Locomotive Works. *Lou Marre collection*

NYC 1334, switching at Charleston, Illinois, in April 1956 is a Class H-5p 2-8-2 built by Brooks in 1917. Mikados ("Mikes") proved to be extremely popular freight locomotives during the steam era in the twentieth century. *Lou Marre collection*

output and maintain high-horsepower at speed without consuming significantly more fuel, Woodard designed an eight-driver locomotive with a substantially larger firebox grate and significantly greater boiler capacity. To support the greater weight of a heavier firebox, the new locomotive required a two-axle articulated rear trailing truck. In 1924 Lima debuted its prototype 2-8-4, the first of what it later called "super power." The locomotive was not significantly larger than NYC's H-10 2-8-2s; it featured 63-inch drivers, 28 x 30-inch cylinders, and weighed 389,000 pounds. It was designed to produce very high horsepower at medium speed.

NYC tested Lima's prototype 2-8-4 in heavy freight service on the steeply graded Boston & Albany line, and the locomotive excelled in this demanding duty. Its vast firebox, with 100 square feet of grate area, allowed the locomotive to burn coal more completely than earlier designs. In tests, the 2-8-4 outperformed the highly successful H-10 Mikado in both pulling power and fuel efficiency. The 2-8-4 generated 69,400 pounds tractive effort compared to an H-10's 63,500 pounds and could develop a total of 82,600 pounds tractive effort with booster. The locomotive was given the designation A-1 to symbolize its superlative qualities and named in honor of the Berkshire hills where it first tested its mettle. Impressed, Cen-

tral ordered 25 Berkshires from Lima in 1926 for the B&A, designating them Class A-1a. Another 20 2-8-4s, Class A-1b, were delivered in 1926 and 1927.

In 1930 NYC ordered ten more Lima Berkshires for the B&A, Class A-1c. With less external plumbing, these locomotives had a noticeably cleaner appearance, the Elesco feedwater heaters having been built into the smoke box and other unsightly plumbing relocated beneath boiler jacketing. As a result, they bore the nickname "sport models." The Berkshire prototype continued to demonstrate its capabilities to other lines around the country and was ultimately sold to the Illinois Central. The Berkshires' featured four-axle radial (hinged) trailing truck soon resulted in a host of new locomotive types, including Central's famous 4-6-4 Hudson.

For 15 years the 55 Berkshires ruled the B&A, handling most freight schedules and rarely working west of Selkirk Yard. However, during World War II some Berks began to wander. Although most remained at home in the hills of Massachusetts, by 1950 diesels had taken over B&A freight assignments and for a short time the Berkshires operated elsewhere on the Central before being sold or scrapped.

In 1948—eighteen years after B&A's last Lima 2-8-4 was delivered—Alco built seven Class A-2a Berkshires for NYC affiliate Pittsburgh & Lake

Erie. These locomotives were heavier than the Lima Berkshires and featured a distinctively large boilers, all-weather cabs, and, like the B&A Berks, 63-inch drivers (most 2-8-4s featured 69-inch drivers). What's interesting about this purchase is that these Berks were delivered after NYC had begun dieselization in earnest, and they were the last domestic steam locomotives built by Alco and NYC's last new steam power. They worked home lines for a few years, but were later transferred to Big Four lines before being retired and scrapped after less than a decade of service.

MOHAWKS

The 4-8-2 was first developed for Chesapeake & Ohio as a passenger locomotive and was soon adapted by other lines as a fast freight hauler. In 1916, New York Central was looking for a better fast freight engine and tested a 4-8-2

in freight service on its Mohawk Division. The railroad was impressed and between 1916 and 1918 ordered 185 4-8-2s from both Alco and Lima. Class as L-1, these locomotives featured 69-inch drivers, 28 x 28-inch cylinders, Walschaerts valve gear, and nearly 67 square feet of firebox grate; they operated at 190 psi boiler pressure and delivered 51,400 pounds tractive effort.

During the mid-1920s, Alco promoted the three-cylinder simple (versus compound) locomotive concept as a way of obtaining greater power and efficiency from a single locomotive. Between 1922 and 1924 NYC explored this idea and Alco rebuilt two L-1s as three-cylinder locomotives. Despite good performance tests, Central decided against more three-cylinder locomotives and chose to order additional Mohawks in a conventional two-cylinder arrangement. Alco delivered the first

Double-headed Berkshire's begin moving their eastbound Boston & Albany freight after taking on water at West Brookfield, Massachusetts, in 1939. The Berkshire name for the 2-8-4 locomotive was inspired by the Massachusetts mountain range of that name in which the prototype 2-8-4 was first tested. J. R. Quinn, Brian Solomon collection

69

On most other railroads, the 4-8-2 was known as a "Mountain," but Central chose to honor the Upstate New York river followed its early predecessors, applying the Indian name Mohawk to its fleet of mighty 4-8-2s. Somewhat weathered, Mohawk No. 3106 is at the Louisville & Nashville locomotive facility at Covington, Kentucky, in 1956, after having delivered a train from Cincinnati across the Ohio River. *John Dziobko*

Class L-2a Mohawks in 1925. Although similar to the L-1 in most respects, the L-2a had 75.3-square-foot firebox grates, 27 x 30-inch cylinders, operated at 225 psi boiler pressure, weighed an additional 21,000 pounds, and featured Elesco feedwater heaters (placed above the headlight) and booster engines. With these improvements the L-2a's produced 60,620 pounds tractive effort—73,280 with booster engine—substantially more power than the L-1s. NYC ordered additional L-2s (L-2b through L-2d) from Alco, delivered in 1929 and 1930.

During the Great Depression traffic when was down, New York Central, along with most American railroads, had surplus power and consequently did not order many new freight locomotives until traffic began to rebound on the eve of World War II. In 1940 and 1941, NYC ordered its third class of Mohawks, 65 dual-service L-3s built by Alco and Lima. They were designed with input gained from experimental modifications on two L-2s and experience from the successful J-3a Hudson. Although these Mohawks were somewhat heavier than the L-2s, they featured a shorter piston stroke, operated at a higher boiler pressure, and used lightweight alloy steel reciprocating parts. Timken roller bearings were used on locomotive wheels and reciprocating parts as well as on most tenders. While they had slightly less tractive effort then the L-2s, they produced

higher maximum drawbar horsepower.

The success of the L-3 led NYC to order its fourth and last class of Mohawk—50 dual-service Class L-4s, all from Lima. Designed for a high-speed, high-horsepower application, they featured 72-inch drivers, 26 x 30-inch cylinders. As the heaviest Mohawks, the L-4a's weighed 396,000 pounds while the L-4b's weighed in at 401,000 pounds. Part of the reason for their greater weight is attributable to wartime restrictions placed on lightweight metals used on the L-3s.

Over more than 25 years, NYC had acquired the largest fleet of 4-8-2s in the nation, some 600 locomotives. Although some of the older L-1s had been retired by the time the new L-3s and L-4s were built, Central's fleet accounted for roughly 25 percent of all the 4-8-2s built for domestic service. They were used in mainline service all over the system, although freight-only Mohawks were typically not assigned to the B&A. Toward the end of steam, Mohawks, like other remaining big steam, were concentrated on Central's western lines.

TEN-WHEELERS AND PRAIRIES

Ten-Wheelers (4-6-0) were employed in a great variety of service all around the New York Central System over a span of more than five decades. Designated Class F (with numerous sub classes), NYC acquired more than 200 of this type between 1899 and 1915 and later inherited more of them with the acquisition of the Ulster & Delaware in the mid 1920s. The Ten-Wheeler enjoyed a brief career as heavy mainline locomotives shortly after the turn of the century and were popular for fast passenger runs west of Buffalo. After 1910, a number were assigned freight duties, particularly on secondary main lines in Upstate New York. In later years, they were concentrated on the Harlem, Putnam, and West Shore lines and worked in both freight and passenger service. Where modern Hudsons, Mohawks, and later Niagaras whisked Central's "Great Steel Fleet" of passenger trains along the Hudson Division main line, an aged Ten-Wheeler trotting along with a short passenger train or a local freight typified late steam operations on lines like the rural, bucolic Putnam Division. Despite their age, some Ten-Wheelers survived into the early 1950s, outlasting many larger, more modern locomotives.

The Prairie type (2-6-2) was not a common wheel arrangement on the NYC but was briefly used by the Lake Shore & Michigan Southern in fast passenger service. Alco built 81 Prairies for the Lake Shore between 1901 and 1905, classed J-40 and J-41. When the Pacific became popular, the brief reign of the Prairie ended and many were scrapped.

ATLANTICS

After the turn of the century, New York Central and its affiliates rapidly acquired a large fleet of high-drivered 4-4-2 Atlantics to supplant 4-4-0s as fast mainline passenger locomotives. Many Atlantics featured 79-inch drivers, and a few were built as compound locomotives (which used a system of high- and low-pressure cylinders to achieve high operating efficiency). The reign of the Atlantic as Central's premier

passenger locomotive was intense, but short. Although the railroad operated 313 Atlantics—using them to handle most passenger assignments between New York and Buffalo—few were ordered after 1907 and by the mid 1930s most had been retired.

PACIFICS

Central's early history with the 4-6-2 Pacific type closely mirrors the application of this standard locomotive on a national scale. NYC was among the first to adopt the Pacific as a passenger locomotive, ordering its first 4-6-2s, Class K, in 1903. NYC ordered additional Pacific's for the B&A and Michigan Central in 1903 and 1904, but it did not embrace the type on a large scale until 1907 when the advent of all-steel passenger equipment, combined with growing passenger business (requiring longer passenger consists), presented a need for more-powerful passenger locomotives. The railroad began to order larger, more-powerful K-2s Pacifics to supplant its Atlantics in fast passenger service. NYC bought 192 K-2s which quickly assumed the role as the railroad's premier passenger locomotive.

In 1910, following experiments with steam superheaters as a way of improving the Pacific's performance, Central ordered a fleet of new superheater-equipped Pacifics from Alco—Class K-3—and proceeded to rebuild its K-2s with superheaters. Simultaneous with the development of the K-3 passenger Pacific, NYC ordered a fleet of K-10, (and later K-11) Pacifics intended for fast freight service. After a few years, these locomotives were bumped from freight work by Mohawks and worked primarily in New York area passenger service, handling secondary passenger trains, local runs, and milk trains.

Lanky Pacific 4704 was built by Schenectady Locomotive Works in 1920 and was classed as a K-3p. With 79-inch drivers, it had no problem keeping schedule with a 10-car passenger train on relatively level main line. However, as passenger cars got heavier and trains became longer, the Pacific would give way to more muscular power on mainline runs. *Ed Crist collection*

Central ordered new K-3s through the early 1920s when it advanced the Pacific design resulting in the K-5 and K-6 Pacifics. The former were equipped with 79-inch drivers for optimum horse power; the latter featured 75-inch drivers for greater tractive effort and assigned them to the steeply graded Boston & Albany. Central's K-5b Pacific could obtain 3,200 maximum drawbar horsepower at 54 mph, and it was this class that led to the designing of an even more powerful locomotive type, Central's famed 4-6-4 Hudson.

HUDSONS

The New York Central served some of the most populous areas of the U.S., and during the boom years of the 1920s its passenger business grew enormously. Even its most powerful Pacifics were straining to maintain the schedules. Central wanted to run longer trains and needed a locomotive that could haul greater loads at sustained high speed, but its abnormally restrictive clearances precluded the design of a Pacific significantly larger than its K-5. The railroad sought another solution. The resounding success of Lima's 2-8-4 Berkshire as an efficient high-horsepower locomotive inspired Central's chief engineer, Paul Kiefer, to develop a six-coupled passenger locomotive with a significantly larger firebox supported by a two-axle radial trailing truck.

Kiefer desired a sleek, balanced, aesthetically pleasing machine, so NYC and Alco worked together and designed a prototype 4-6-4—Class J-1a, No. 5200. Delivered in February 1927, it met all of its intended design criteria and was named in honor of the Hudson River so closely associated with the New York Central. It featured 79-inch drivers and 25 x 28-inch cylinders—the same as Central's K-5 Pacifics—but employed an 81.5-square-foot firebox grate (roughly 20 percent larger than the Pacific) and operated at 225 psi boiler pressure. Appliances, such as an Elesco feedwater heater and other plumbing were neatly tucked within the locomotive body to satisfy Kiefer's aesthetical considerations. In tests, the handsome locomotive produced 28 percent greater maximum horsepower than the K-5 and 1,600 pounds greater tractive effort.

The Hudson was precisely what the railroad needed and it promptly ordered a great

fleet: 205 J-1s, built between 1927 and 1931. Later J-1s featured additional improvements such as Baker valve gear, cast steel frames, and larger tenders. NYC ordered 20 Class J-2 Hudsons for the Boston & Albany built by Alco and Lima between 1928 and 1931. Like the K-6 Pacific, the J-2 employed 75-inch drivers.

In 1935, NYC refined its already very successful Hudson, ordering a fleet of 50 J-3a "super Hudsons" that featured a variety of modifications to improve performance and efficiency. Cylinder stroke was shortened to 22.5 inches and the bore increased by 1 inch to 29 inches; boiler pressure was raised to 275 psi. Aluminum was used for running boards, cabs, and other non-essential equipment to limit the total weight of the locomotive. Lightweight alloy steel was used for piston rods, main rods, and other reciprocat-

ing parts, reducing the dynamic augment that was especially severe at high speeds. Instead of traditional spoked wheels, the Hudsons used "boxpok" and "Scullin disc" designs. Timken roller bearings, which had been experimentally applied to eight J-1 Hudsons, were used on all J-3a's. Roller bearings were used on all locomotive wheels and tenders.

Although the J-3a's refinements may seem relatively minor, they were very effective, resulting in one of the most efficient steam locomotives ever designed. The J-3a produced a maximum of 4,725 hp at 75 mph; 875 more horsepower than produced by the J-1 and achieved at slightly higher speed. The J-3a used less coal and water than J-1s and had one of the best reliability and service records of any NYC locomotive. They regularly ran more than 20,000 miles per month. The J-3a was the zenith of the six-coupled steam locomotive and the Hudson in general became one of the most lasting symbols of the New York Central.

NIAGARAS

Central was among the last American railroads to adopt the 4-8-4 type on a wide scale, but its 4-8-4s—known as "Niagaras" rather than the more common moniker "Northern"—were among the finest examples of the 4-8-4. Although NYC experimented with an unorthodox, extremely high-pressure, three-cylinder compound 4-8-4 in 1930, its 4-8-4s built 15 years later were actually an expansion of its 4-8-2 Mohawk type that also incorporated technology refined on the 4-6-4 Hudson.

At the end of World War II, when most American railroads looked toward dieselization, Central believed traditional reciprocating steam locomotives might still prove to be a competitive motive-power solution and designed a prototype 4-8-4 intended for high-speed passenger service and fast freight service. This locomotive—No. 6000, Class S-1a—was built by Alco in August 1945. It featured an enormous boiler, built to the limits of

NYC system clearances, and was too large to incorporate a steam dome and so instead used a steam dry pipe for steam collection. Boiler pressure was 290 psi, and the firebox had a 100-square-foot grate, 24.7 square feet larger than the L-4 Mohawk. Like the J-3a Hudsons and some late-era Mohawks, the Niagara employed lightweight alloy steel reciprocating parts. Main rods were made from manganese-vanadium steel. The cab and other non-essential parts were made from aluminum, while the frame was made of cast steel with integral cylinders to minimize the weight of the locomotive. All wheels and reciprocating parts were equipped with Timken roller bearings to ensure minimum resistance and reduce the chance of on-line failure. The tender featured a two-axle leading truck followed by five axles rigidly attached in centipede fashion. In tests the machine proved its merit. Initially it was equipped with 75-inch drivers, but these were soon replaced with 79-inch drivers. The loco-

One of Central's classic Hudsons drifts toward Cincinnati Union Terminal with the overnight Big Four train from Chicago in the late 1950s. Few steam locomotives commanded such a burly yet well-proportioned appearance. Enthralled by these big machines, electric toy-train manufacturers American Flyer and Lionel offered model Hudsons to countless Baby Boomers. *Alvin Schultz*

THE STREAMLINED HUDSON

Underneath all the shrouding of the locomotive *Commodore Vanderbilt* is a standard J-class 4-6-4 Hudson. The *Commodore* was streamlined to reduce wind resistance and therefore save fuel, however the shroudwork greatly hampered maintenance and negated such benefits. The locomotive (Hudson 5344 in disguise) later received a more modest streamlining treatment. *Lou Marre collection*

In the 1930s streamlining was the wave of the future, and New York Central led the way in streamlined steam locomotive design. Donald J. Bush, author of *The Streamline Decade*, indicates that Norman Zapf, an engineering graduate student at the Case School of Applied Science in Cleveland, performed wind-tunnel tests showing that streamlined shrouds would reduce wind drag by more than 90 percent and improve locomotive output. Zapf used a New York Central Hudson for his model and presented his design research to the New York Central.

In December 1934 NYC applied streamlined, wind-resistant shrouds to J-1 Hudson No. 5344 using a design credited to the railroad's Carl F. Kantola, an engineer in the Equipment Design Department. Though not the first streamlined train, this was the first streamlined steam locomotive in America. Named *Commodore Vanderbilt*, it resembled an upside-down bathtub and was assigned to power Central's premier *20th Century Limited*. Although streamlined steam locomotives became relatively popular in the 1930s and 1940s, the *Commodore*'s shrouding application was relatively short-lived. Its sheet metal covered most of the locomotive's working machinery, dramatically increasing maintenance costs that offset any advantages obtained through improved performance. NYC 5344 was later recovered with more aesthetically pleasing shrouds, making it one of the only steam locomotives to receive two different streamlining treatments. New York

Central later applied other more visually pleasing and maintenance-friendly streamlining treatments to its fast passenger locomotives.

In conjunction with the 1938 inauguration of the Henry Dreyfuss-designed streamlined *20th Century Limited*, ten J-3a Hudsons were delivered with sophisticated streamlined shrouds. Unlike other aesthetically motivated designs that incorporated a potpourri of complex embellishments and unnecessary adornment, Dreyfuss' design excelled in its sublime simplicity and functionality. Except for a radial fin that bisected the nose of the locomotive, Dreyfuss' streamlining cleaned up the lines of the locomotive without disguising or hiding the bulk of the machinery in what the designer himself described as "cleanlining." This made for a locomotive of outstanding good looks and minimal maintenance interference.

The Dreyfuss Hudson was one of the finest designs of the entire streamlined era and remains of the best-remembered and most-recognized modern locomotives. It was prominently featured in New York Central advertising and has been pictured again and again in books, magazines, and even in random railroad-related "public" art over the years— including on 1970s-era polyester dress shirts. "Rolling Power," the famous painting by renowned Precisionist artist Charles Sheeler, featured a Dreyfuss Hudson's Scullin disc drivers. In 1999 the United States Post Office issued a series of commemorative railroad stamps, one of which portrayed the Dreyfuss Hudson—a locomotive which had become an icon of the halcyon days of the New York Central System.

Though the shrouding application was much more restrained on the ten *Century* Hudsons (also used on the *20th Century Limited's* running mates, the *Commodore Vanderbilt* and *Advance Commodore Vanderbilt*), the effect was much more dazzling and stylish. Absent was the overinflated appearance harbored by the *Commodore Vanderbilt* Hudson; now bystanders could witness the fury of whirling drivers and blurring rod action as the *Centurys* passed in the night. And, it cut down on the cursing from maintenance crews. *Andover Junction Publications Archives*

motive produced 62,400 pounds maximum tractive effort and delivered 6,000 maximum-drawbar horsepower (performance revealed by its distinctive road number). It could haul an 18-car passenger train at a sustained 80 mph without straining. Central hoped its performance would match that of Electro-Motive's new E-series passenger diesels.

The railroad ordered another 26 Niagaras in 1945 and 1946. Twenty-five were Class S-1b's and in most respects resembled the prototype. Their tractive effort was slightly less that the S-1a and only operated at 275 psi. The last locomotive, Class S-2a, featured Franklin rotary-cam actuated poppet valves, instead of the more conventional piston valves and Baker valve gear. Like some of the Mohawks, the Niagaras were equipped with "elephant ear" smoke lifters to deflect smoke away from the cab when the locomotives were operating at speed. The Niagaras did match the performance of the EMD E-unit, regularly running more than 25,000 miles a month. However, the Niagara did so at much greater cost. They were soon bumped by diesels, and within a decade they were gone.

SWITCHERS, HUMP ENGINES AND MALLETS

The Central operated a large fleet of 0-6-0, (Class B), and 0-8-0 (Class U) switchers. The vast majority of these locomotives were built by Alco, however there were a few exceptions. Lima built 20 0-6-0s, and a number of 0-8-0s. NYC constructed some of its own 0-8-0s at company shops, notably 11 Class U-33s at B&A's West Springfield (Massachusetts) Shops and 20 U-60s at Big Four's Beech Grove complex near Indianapolis. Between 1905 and 1909 NYC acquired a fleet of Class M 0-10-0 switchers for slow-speed hump-yard service.

In 1913 NYC and its affiliates began acquiring a small fleet of articulated Mallet compounds for yard service. The railroad had a sole 0-6-6-0, Class NB-1a, and a handful of 0-8-8-0s, Class NU-1a through NU-1e, that worked in hump service system wide. Some of these locomotives survived as compounds until the mid-1940s, a decade after most Mallets in the U.S. had either been converted to simple articulated locomotives (which used high-pressure steam in both sets of cylinders, instead of the compound system

Chunky 0-8-0 No. 7796 rests between chores at Kankakee, Illinois, in February 1956. *Monty Powell*

that used high-pressure cylinders that exhausted into low-pressure cylinders for greater efficiency).

Central had a fleet of Mallets for road service as well. In 1910 it purchased a 2-6-6-2, Class NE-1a, for service on the west end of the B&A. In 1913 NYC ordered additional 2-6-6-2s, Class NE-2 in 1911 for the B&A and for its rugged Pennsylvania routes. The B&A Mallets were primarily used as helpers but were also used to lead freights; they were retired in the early 1930s, a few years after the A-1 Berkshires assumed most mainline freight duties. The railroad's last 2-6-6-2s were delivered in 1921, bringing its roster of 2-6-6-2s to 74. Some Mallets were later transferred to Ohio where they served in heavy freight service on secondary lines until the early 1950s. All NYC Mallets were built by Alco, the company that first adapted the type for American service in 1904 for the Baltimore & Ohio.

SUBURBAN TANKS

New York Central maintained two fleets of tank locomotives for suburban passenger service in New York City and on the B&A in Boston. These locomotives did not feature a separate tender and were designed to operate bidirectionally with a train at low speed. The oldest tanks were 0-4-4T used on the New York & Harlem that dated from the 1870s. Class J 2-6-6Ts were built for New York City service by Alco in 1901 and were transferred to Boston following electrification of the New York suburban lines. In the late 1920s and 1930s they were rebuilt and reclassed D-2. The largest tanks were B&A's 4-6-6T Class D-1s, built by Alco in 1928. Resembling Central's Hudsons in appearance, they featured 23.5 x 26-inch cylinders and 63-inch drivers and weighed 352,000 pounds. B&A's tanks were primarily used on commuter trains on both the Highland branch and the main line between Boston and Riverside, Massachusetts.

Mallet 9091 at McKees Rocks, Pennsylvania, was one of two 0-8-8-0s built for the Pittsburgh & Lake Erie by Brooks Locomotive Works. These were the only Mallets built for the P&LE. *C. W. Burns, collection of Herbert H. Harwood Jr.*

Clean and shiny, New York Central Electro-Motive F7s stand proud at the West Detroit, Michigan, locomotive servicing facility in 1961. Though subdued in terms of color, Central's lightning stripe diesel scheme—be it the two-tone gray as used on passenger locomotives or the black and gray as shown here—was one of the classiest liveries of steam-to-diesel transition-era railroading. *Hank Goerke*

DIESEL LOCOMOTIVES OF THE NEW YORK CENTRAL SYSTEM

Central's Far-Flung Diesel Fleet Featured Wide Variety

New York Central was among the earliest users of diesel-electric locomotives, acquiring experimental diesel power in the late 1920s. Its first large fleet of diesels were unique Alco-General Electric tri-power locomotives built in 1928 and 1930 and designed for switching service in Manhattan. The story was different for over-the-road passenger and freight diesels, though. When many American railroads began acquiring diesel-electrics for passenger service in the mid-1930s and then Electro-Motive's pioneering road freight FT diesels in the late 1930s and early 1940s, Central chose to rely principally on conventional steam locomotives (and electrics into Grand Central) for its through trains until after World War II. Despite NYC's diesel dabblings for switching service in the 1920s and 1930s, the railroad was not convinced that diesels represented the most efficient mainline motive power solution.

Toward the end of the war, NYC investigated road diesels, purchasing FT road freight diesels in 1944 and, for passenger service, Electro-Motive E7s in 1945. However, the Central was still not fully convinced and continued to refine its steam fleet and develop its highly efficient 4-8-4 Niagara in 1945 and 1946 (see chapter 5). By late 1946, despite extraordinary efforts to refine the reciprocating steam locomotive in order to equal diesel-electric performance, the railroad finally conceded that diesel-electrics were a more economical solution than even the most modern steam locomotives and ordered large numbers of new diesels for road service.

Central's largest orders went to dominant diesel builder EMD (General Motors' Electro-Motive Division), with significant orders also placed with its long-time locomotive supplier, Alco. Early in its dieselization NYC also purchased some diesels from Baldwin, Lima-Hamilton, and Fairbanks-Morse. However, by the mid-1950s difficulties with the designs of these three minority builders and improved locomotives from EMD and Alco discouraged NYC from placing additional orders with Baldwin, L-H, and F-M. Central's dieselization was completed in 1957 when the railroad ceased operating steam and had phased out electric operation of its New York freight lines, Cleveland Union Terminal, and Detroit River Tunnel.

In 1957, a nationwide recession caused a serious drop in freight traffic. This, combined with NYC's decision to scale back passenger operations, left the railroad with sufficient motive power for several years. Many passenger locomotives were bumped into freight service, and some older locomotives were retired. In the early 1960s, the railroad further streamlined its diesel fleet as it began acquiring new high-horsepower locomotives—first from EMD and Alco in 1961 and 1962, and then from General Electric beginning in

1964—allowing it to dispose of old, unusual, and poorly performing locomotives. By the mid-1960s most unusual models, including pre-war locomotives from Electro-Motive and Alco and most Baldwin, Fairbanks-Morse, and Lima products, including those that Central had rebuilt with EMD prime movers, were stricken from the roster.

In its time, New York Central operated one of the largest diesel fleets in the nation. Its all-time diesel roster, including subsidiaries and affiliated lines, lists 2,751 locomotives. NYC operated an unusually eclectic fleet, which included locomotives from six different diesel builders and a great variety of models, including a multitude of rare types used only on a few

railroads, such as Baldwin's "shark nose" cabs and Fairbanks-Morse passenger C-Liner cabs.

Although the railroad operated a large fleet of six-axle passenger cabs with A-1-A trucks (wheel assemblies with two powered axles and an unpowered center "idler" axle), it did not own any "six-motor" diesels (diesels with two "C" trucks each with three powered axles), and ignored the nationwide trend toward high-horsepower six-motor locomotives in the 1960s. This decision has been attributed to Central's largely grade-less, "water level" profile, although it seems inconsistent with the railroad's steam-era philosophy to operate specialized high-tractive effort locomotives on its grade-intensive Boston & Albany line.

Once dieselization was underway, NYC made a concerted effort to keep like locomotives in designated pools and usually based them near a home repair terminal. As locomotives aged and new classes were delivered, it was common for the railroad to reassign whole classes of locomotives from one region to another. Despite its pooling practice, it was not unusual for locomotives to stray and wander around the system.

While Central's roster was certainly diverse, it was not particularly colorful. Black, white, and various shades of gray were the dominant dress over the years. Prior to World War II, most NYC diesels were painted black, with small white lettering and numbers in the same fashion as its electric locomotives. A few switchers were painted gray. Early EMD road locomotives featured experimental schemes, but in the mid-1940s the hallmark NYC two-tone gray, 'lightning stripe' scheme with the classy crimson herald became the standard dress for most road diesels. Most switchers still wore basic black, although some wore NYC heralds in addition to lettering. About 1960, the railroad adopted a new, simplified scheme—essentially all black with a white stripe and a new streamlined logo. A few locomotives wore variations to this scheme, substituting dark gray for black, or the case of three EMD E units, "Century green" for black. Another experiment substituted a gold stripe for the white one, but still used white logo.

ALCO

During the steam era the American Locomotive Company was Central's largest locomotive supplier. Alco and General Electric had cooperated in building many NYC third-rail electrics, and this consortium also built Central's first diesels. In the early years of its dieselization, the railroad also relied heavily upon Alco-GE for its diesel-electric fleet. NYC operated a total of 770 Alco diesels (although not all were on the roster at the same time), one of the largest rosters of Alco diesels in North America. NYC continued to purchase Alco diesels after Alco and GE dissolved their

NYC 1561 was one of 42 "tri-power" (diesel-electric/battery/ straight electric) locomotives built in 1928 and 1930 by Alco, General Electric, and Ingersoll-Rand. The units were primarily intended for switching service around New York City, but two units, Nos. 1561 and 1562, were built minus third-rail pickup shoes and were assigned to Chicago. The 1561 is shown at La Salle Street Station, date unknown. *Cal's Classics*

Alco's S-series switchers were popular with a number of railroads. The 9756 was an Alco model S-4 (Class DES-11L on the Central) built in 1953 for the Pittsburgh & Lake Erie. Unit 9756 is working the old Spuyten Duyvil & Port Morris line in the Bronx.

Central owned the largest fleet of Alco's FA/B-series freight-cab locomotives of any U.S. railroad—197 units in both A (cab) and B (booster) configuration. They were delivered in the late 1940s and early 1950s, about the same time as the competition—Electro-Motive's later-model (post FT) F-series freight diesels. *Hank Goerke*

cooperative arrangement in 1953. Meanwhile GE went on to develop its own line of road diesels in competition with Alco, and New York Central would become a prominent GE diesel customer.

Although the Central remained loyal to the traditional locomotive builder in later years (its last new diesel-electrics were 10 Alco Century 430s built in 1967, just a year before New York Central merged with the Pennsylvania Railroad, and only two years before Alco exited domestic locomotive production), the railroad placed the majority of its locomotive orders at this time with EMD and GE, Alco's principal competitors.

In 1928 Alco-GE built two experimental box-cabs (one is often credited as the first road diesel in the United States), which performed long-term tests on the NYC. Then, between 1928 and 1930, Central acquired a fleet of 42 tri-power (diesel-electric/straight electric/battery) locomotives from the Alco-GE-Ingersoll Rand consortium for service on the new West Side Freight Line (see chapter 9). The prototype was a center-cab, but the remaining 41 locomotives employed a box-cab configuration. They were equipped with a six-cylinder 300-horsepower Ingersoll Rand engine, a bank

of high-power batteries, and third-rail shoes. They were capable of working from any of these power sources. Most held assignments as switchers in Manhattan, although four were built for Michigan Central and worked in the Detroit area. Some tri-power locomotives also served in Chicago and Boston. After NYC discontinued its electrified freight operations, the tri-power locomotives were no longer needed and the entire fleet was retired by the end of 1958.

Beginning in the late 1930s, Central acquired a small fleet of Alco HH660 ("high hood," 660 horsepower) diesel-electric switchers. Five were assigned to the Boston & Albany and were the only diesels lettered for B&A. The others were initially assigned to the Buffalo area. Between 1940 and 1953, the railroad assembled a fleet of 282 Alco S-series switchers, which worked as yard goats and local locomotives all across the system.

In 1947 and 1948 Alco built 44 FA1 cabs, and 23 FB1 boosters for NYC. Designed for heavy-freight service, each unit produced 1,500 horsepower. Another 80 FA2 cabs and 50 FB2 boosters, rated at 1,600 horsepower each, followed in 1951 and 1952, giving Central the largest fleet of Alco freight cabs. In their early

Twenty of Alco's handsome PA/B-series passenger locomotives graced NYC's diesel roster—far less than Electro-Motive's competing E-series models. Though aesthetically pleasing in terms of their timeless design, Alco's PAs were beset with mechanical problems and relatively few were sold. This A-B set is about to take an early evening train—possibly the *Lake Shore Limited*—out of Chicago in 1950. *Cal's Classics*

NYC 8000 was one of nine Alco RS11 road-switchers (Class DRS-10 on the Central) delivered in 1957 and was the first road-switcher to carry NYC's solid black diesel scheme with large white lettering. At the time of delivery, these locomotives also featured the railroad's short-lived "script" herald. As with most Eastern railroads, Central operated its high-hood road-switchers long-end forward, so this view technically shows the back end of the locomotive. The 1,800-horsepower RS11 was followed by its 2,000-horsepower cousin, the RS32 (ClassDRS-12 on NYC), of which the railroad acquired 25 units in 1961-62, all with low noses. *Lou Marre*

years, the FAs primarily worked east of Cleveland and were commonly assigned to through freights along the Water Level Route main line, on the West Shore, and B&A.

In the same time frame as the freight cabs, Central also acquired a fleet of 20 Alco PA/PB passenger cabs and boosters. Four were assigned to the Pittsburgh & Lake Erie, but the remainder worked in the passenger pool with the EMD E units. These Alcos suffered from performance and reliability problems attributed to the new-model engine that Alco had used in them; consequently most were retired in the early 1960s prior to their EMD peers.

Central operated a substantial fleet of Alco road-switchers consisting of 14 1,000-horsepower RS1s and 23 1,500-horsepower RS2s acquired between 1948 and 1950; 135 1,600-horsepower RS3s acquired between 1950 and 1953; 9 1,800-horsepower RS11s in 1957 (part of an order of 15, some of which eventually went to the Delaware & Hudson); 25 2,000-horsepower RS32s delivered in 1961 and 1962; and finally 10 Century-series 430s—Alco's late-era high-horsepower road-switcher. Many of the RS2s and RS3s worked in local and secondary passenger service on eastern routes. In their early years some RS2s were assigned to the B&A and worked on suburban runs out of Boston South Station or handled branchline locals. The RS32s and C430s were intended for fast freight service and worked in mainline service, usually on New York State routes.

Central dabbled with diesel switchers for many years before conceding that diesel-electric technology really would work well in heavy-duty, over-the-road freight service. Its first road diesels were four A-B sets of Electro-Motive's pioneering FT locomotives, delivered in 1944. Central would quickly embrace the F-unit and order dozens of post-FT models—341 to be exact.

NYC's first passenger diesels were Electro-Motive E7s. Although many other railroads had begun dieselizing their passenger services in the 1930s and early 1940s, Central did not take delivery of the first E7s until 1945, but it did so in a big way: By the end of 1949, 50 E7s were roaming the system, hauling mainline intercity trains from the *20th Century Limited* on down. *EMD*

The E7 was superceded by the E8 in Electro-Motive's catalog in 1949, and in 1951 NYC began taking delivery of its first batch of E8s. By 1954, NYC had 60 E8s on the property—interestingly only A-units, no boosters. Unit 4053, shown at Detroit in 1961, was built in 1952. Although delivered in Central's dashing two-tone gray lightning stripe scheme, this unit and two other E-units, one of which is the E7 coupled to the 4053 in this scene, for a short time in the 1960s wore an experimental scheme that featured Central's new "Mercury Green" (jade green) color that was appearing on new freight rolling stock of that period.

ELECTRO MOTIVE

Following World War II, General Motor's Electro Motive Division, the dominant American diesel locomotive builder, became New York Central's primary locomotive supplier. NYC first sampled the builder's products in 1936 when its Chicago River & Indiana subsidiary took delivery seven Electro-Motive Corporation (which became Electro-Motive Division in 1941) 600-horsepower SC locomotives that used Winton diesel engines. These locomotives proved successful, and over the years numerous orders for EMD switchers followed. By 1955 Central had acquired 483 EMC/EMD switchers. An additional 22 SW1500 switchers were built in the late 1960s for NYC/Milwaukee Road subsidiary Indiana Harbor Belt.

NYC sampled Electro-Motive's acclaimed FT road diesels in 1944 when it took delivery of eight FT freight cabs (four "A-unit" cabs and four cabless "B-unit" boosters). This revolutionary model had been on the market since 1939 and by the mid 1940s had demonstrated exceptional efficiency. Employing EMD's 567 engine—a two-stroke engine model that improved upon the Winton design—each locomotive developed 1350 horsepower and were typically operated in two- or four-unit sets using either an A-B or A-B-B-A configuration. Despite

EMD's excellent track record, Central still approached the road diesel concept cautiously and spent roughly two years evaluating the FTs' performance before ordering additional road freight cabs. While the FT was succeeded by more advanced F-series units, NYC ultimately found the locomotive's performance satisfactory and over a five-year span beginning in 1947, the railroad amassed a fleet of 341 F-units (1,350-horsepower F2s and 1,500-horsepower F3 and F7 cabs and boosters), including a small fleet dual-service (freight and passenger) F3s.

Simultaneous with the railroad's evaluation of the F-unit, it ordered EMD's E7 passenger cabs, which featured twin 567 prime movers that generated 2,000 horsepower and rode on two A-1-A trucks. The E-units performed superbly and in a short time displaced Central's highly acclaimed Hudsons and recently introduced Niagaras from premier passenger runs. NYC acquired 50 E7 (36 cabs and 14 boosters) between 1945 and 1949, followed by 60 2,250-horsepower E8A cabs between 1951 and 1953. The E-units remained in passenger service system wide through the New York Central era, and many survived not only into Penn Central, but into the early years of Amtrak. They were also assigned to mail and express trains, and then in the mid-1960s were

The first "second-generation" locomotives—high-horsepower units designed to replace postwar-era locomotives being retired—that NYC acquired from Electro-Motive were 15 low-nose GP20s (NYC Class DRS-11), delivered in 1961. A year later, Central began taking delivery of 25 Electro-Motive GP30s (NYC Class DRS-13), one of which rides tall and proud across the Great Miami River in Dayton, Ohio, in 1970. Two years after the Penn Central merger, the unit was still wearing its NYC livery. *David P. Oroszi*

assigned fast freight service duties, often hauling Super Van trains.

New York Central completed its systemwide dieselization with the acquisition of EMD's highly successful "General Purpose" road switchers. Between 1950 and 1953 EMD delivered 228 1,500-horsepower GP7s followed by 176 1,750-horsepower GP9s between 1954 and 1957. Many "Geeps" (pronounced "jeeps") were designed for dual-purpose service, equipped with steam-generators (for train heat) and high-speed gearing so they could work passenger trains.

In the 1960s NYC ordered EMD's new high-horsepower road-switchers beginning with 15 2,000-horsepower GP20s in 1961; this was followed by 10 2,250-horsepower GP30s in 1962 and 31 2,500-horsepower GP35s between 1963 and 1965. EMD introduced its new, more-powerful 645 prime mover in the mid-1960s, and New York Central took delivery of 105 3,000-horsepower GP40s that used the new engine. All high-horsepower road-switchers were designed for mainline fast freight service

and served in this capacity system wide, displacing numerous older locomotives including Central's vast fleet of F units. Central's primary EMD shop was at Collinwood Yard in Cleveland, and although EMDs roamed the entire system, they were more prevalent on western lines then in the East where Alcos and GEs dominated.

BALDWIN

Baldwin had been the foremost steam locomotive builder in the United States. It entered the diesel-electric market later than Alco and EMD and did not begin producing road diesels until after World War II. Ultimately Baldwin found itself unable to compete with EMD and exited the locomotive business in 1956.

NYC did not purchase large numbers of Baldwin steam locomotives, yet in the early years of dieselization, the railroad sampled a variety of Baldwin diesels. Nonetheless, Central only owned 99 Baldwin diesels, so for every Baldwin, NYC had nearly eight Alcos and more than 15 EMD units. NYC's Baldwin fleet

Baldwin RS4-4-15 No. 7300 was one of only two such units on the NYC, the mate being 7301. Built in 1948, the pair were re-engined with Electro-Motive power plants in 1956. The units were a fixture in the Chicago area for a number of years; the 7300 is shown switching at La Salle Street Station with Electro-Motive SW1 switcher 672 in 1962. *Hank Goerke*

Although originally intended for Chicago–Boston passenger service, NYC's Baldwin "Babyface" DR6-4-15s did not perform to expectations. Central had six of these unusual locomotives (Class DC), four A-units and two B-units. They were built in 1947-48, re-engined in 1955, and scrapped in 1962. They were referred to by NYC crews as "Gravel Gerties." The 3507 is shown coupled to an F3B at Cincinnati in 1956. *John Dziobko*

Baldwin's RF16 (for Road Freight, 1,600 horsepower) model locomotives were meant to compete with Electro-Motive's F-series and Alco's FA/FB models. Central's 26 RF16s, in both cab and booster configurations, were built in 1951-52 served the Central as late as 1967 when a number of them were sold off to the Monongahela Railroad. *Collection of Tim Doherty*

was eclectic and diverse, featuring some of Baldwin's more interesting models. However, poor performance and incompatibility with other builders plagued Central's Baldwin fleet, and by the mid-1960s most had been retired.

The majority of NYC's Baldwin diesels were switchers. It purchased a dozen 600-horsepower DS4-4-6s during World War II and continued to buy Baldwin switchers until 1952. Following the war, Central made a few token purchases of Baldwin road diesels. In 1947 and 1948 it acquired 12 1,500-horsepower Baldwin "Babyface" cab units: six DR4-4-15s with B-B trucks (two-axle trucks, both axles powered) designed for freight service and six DR6-4-15s with six-axle A-1-A trucks intended for dual service. These later cabs acquired the derogatory moniker "Gravel Gerties" and were unpopular with both the railroad and train crews. The only other line to purchase DR6-4-15s was Seaboard Air Line. In their early years these Baldwin cabs often hauled passenger trains on the B&A and were regularly assigned to the *Paul Revere* and *New England States*. Later they were also used on the Hudson line. In addition to the cabs, Baldwin in 1948 delivered a pair of RS4-4-15 road-switchers.

In 1951 and 1952, following the merger between Baldwin and Lima-Hamilton, Baldwin delivered its last road freight locomotives to New York Central—26 RF16 "shark nose" cabs and boosters and 17 RS12 1,200-horsepower road-switchers. Central's very last Baldwin (and one of the last locomotives Baldwin constructed) was a sole RP210H sharknose-style diesel-hydraulic power unit for the ill-fated experimental lightweight streamliner, The Xplorer. Built in 1956, the unit wore a unique blue-and-yellow paint scheme and stood only 11 feet tall, making it significantly shorter than most modern American diesel locomotives. The low-slung locomotive and its Talgo-style train were retired in 1960 and sold to the Pickens Railroad.

FAIRBANKS-MORSE

Diesel engine manufacturer Fairbanks-Morse entered the diesel-electric locomotive market at the end of World War II, and New York Central bought 119 Fairbanks-Morse locomotives between 1946 and 1952. The F-M engine used an opposed piston design that employed two pistons facing each other in each cylinder. The advantage was that it produced significantly more horsepower than an EMD, Alco, or Baldwin engine of same cylinder count. In the late 1940s, F-M introduced 2,000- and 2-400-horsepower locomotives—more than a decade before other builders achieved the same power in single-engined locomotives. However, while the F-M opposed-piston engine had performed well in marine and industrial applications, it was not widely embraced in the

Two Fairbanks-Morse "Eries" burst out of La Salle Street Station with the Toledo local on March 24, 1954. Built for F-M at General Electric's plant at Erie, Pennsylvania (hence the "Erie" or "Erie-Built" monikers often applied to this locomotive model), in 1949, the 2,000-horsepower Eries tended to be reserved for passenger runs of lesser esteem—as seemed to be the case for nearly all of NYC's oddball passenger diesels. *Eugene Van Dusen, Bill Eley collection*

locomotive field. F-M locomotives were saddled with exceptionally high maintenance costs and as a result had comparatively short service lives. NYC rebuilt some of its F-Ms in the mid-1950s with EMD engines, but even these locomotives were withdrawn from service by the mid-1960s.

NYC acquired 11 1,000-horsepower H10-44 and 27 1,200-horsepower H12-44 switchers between 1946 and 1952. These locomotives, along with 13 1,600-horsepower H16-44 road-switchers bought in the same period were attractively styled by famed industrial designer Raymond Loewy and were delivered in Central's two-tone gray lightning-stripe paint scheme. In 1948 and 1949, F-M built 19 2,000-horsepower H20-44 road-switchers used by New York Central and its affiliated lines.

NYC operated one of the most diverse fleets of Fairbanks-Morse cab units. A fleet of 14 2,000-horsepower "Eries" or "Erie-builts" (so named because the car bodies were erected at General Electric's Erie, Pennsylvania, shops) were delivered between 1947 and 1949. Of these, six were geared for 97 miles per hour and intended for passenger service while the remainder were geared for 79 miles per hour and intended for fast freight service. These locomotives were 64 feet long and rode on A-1-A trucks. The freight Erie's were typically assigned to Pacemaker freights, and it was not uncommon to find a single Erie cab racing along with a train of red and gray Pacemaker cars.

In 1950 and 1952, F-M delivered 35 C-liner cabs: 8 2,400-horsepower CPA24-4 (with an unusual B–A-1-A wheel arrangement for passenger service); 8 1,600-horsepower CPA16-4 (cabs) and three CPB16-4 (boosters) with a B-B truck arrangement for passenger service; and 12 2,000-horsepower CFA-20-4 (cabs) and three CFB-20-4 (boosters) in a B-B arrangement for freight service.

When new, many F-M cabs worked on the Boston & Albany. Central felt the high-horsepower locomotives were well suited to B&A's grades, and in the late 1940s and early 1950s, F-Ms were the most common type of motive power operating on the route. Later they were displaced by Alcos.

LIMA-HAMILTON

In the late 1940s steam-locomotive manufacturer Lima Locomotive merged with diesel-engine producer Hamilton Corporation forming Lima-Hamilton. Between 1949 and 1951 the company produced 174 diesel-electric locomotives before merging with Baldwin and discontinuing its locomotive line; Lima diesels were therefore among the rarest in America. New York Central was one of Lima-Hamilton's largest customers and acquired 49 L-H diesel-electrics. Although most of these were switchers, there was also a small fleet of 16 1,200-horsepower dual-service road switchers that came equipped with steam generators, necessary for train heating when the locomotives were used in passenger service. NYC was the sole owner of this unique type, which were delivered in the lightning-stripe livery and bore a strong resemblance to Alco's RS1. Initially Central assigned most of these road locomotives to secondary passenger runs on the B&A. Later some worked B&A local and branchline freights and New York City area passenger runs on the West Shore, Harlem, and Putnam lines. In the mid-1950s they were sent west to work in Big Four territory. NYC rebuilt two of the 1,200-horsepower road switchers at its Collinwood Shops with EMD 12-cylinder 567 engines, and the pair became a fixture shunting passenger equipment

between Chicago's La Salle Street Station and the Central's passenger yard at 43rd Street. All of the unrebuilt 1,200-horsepower road-switchers along with most of switchers were retired by 1966 while the two EMD re-powered locomotives survived into the Penn Central era.

GENERAL ELECTRIC

General Electric had been involved with the development of diesel-electric locomotives since the 1920s, and in addition to road locomotives built in partnership with Alco, it also produced its own switching locomotives. New York Central owned several small, GE center-cab switchers, including a particularly early locomotive originally built for Eastman Kodak about 1923. In the 1950s, following the dissolution of the, Alco-GE partnership, GE developed its own line of high-horsepower road diesels using the Cooper-Bessemer four-stroke 16-cylinder FDL diesel engine.

GE's "Universal Line" debuted with the 2,500-horsepower U25B in the late 1950s, and in 1964-65 NYC took delivery of 70 U25Bs. (For obvious reasons, GE's Universal-series locomotives soon acquired the widespread nickname "U-Boats," a term which survives to this day.) In 1966 GE built 24 2800-horsepower U28Bs for the New York Central System, 22 of which were delivered to the Pittsburgh & Lake Erie (and so lettered) in the distinctive U25B carbody (bulbous protruding short low nose). They remained P&LE locomotives following the Penn Central merger. Central's last GE's were 60 3,000-horsepower U30Bs, delivered in 1967, one of which is shown on page 111.

New York Central went for General Electric motive power in a big way once GE got into locomotive manufacturing on its own in the late 1950s. The railroad began with 70 2,500-horsepower U25Bs delivered in 1964-65, and then in 1966 took delivery of 24 U28Bs; 22 were lettered for Pittsburgh & Lake Erie, as illustrated by units 2814 and 2808 in 1966. *Jim Boyd*

93

Quiet, clean, and functional, New York Central's electric locomotives moved passenger trains through urban areas and tunnels for more than half of the twentieth century. On October 17, 1959, a Class P-2 motor slides into Crestwood station on the Harlem Division. *Richard J. Solomon*

8

ELECTRIC LOCOMOTIVES OF THE NEW YORK CENTRAL

Electric Motive Power for New York, Cleveland, and Detroit

New York Central was among the earliest railroads to explore mainline electrification (see chapter 5), and Central maintained a substantial fleet of electric "motors" —as electric locomotives are often called—for its New York City electrified lines and smaller fleets for its Cleveland Union Terminal and Detroit River Tunnel electrifications. While most American railroads used a system of overhead electrification whereby current was collected from catenary (overhead wire) by pantographs mounted on the locomotive roof, Central's New York City and Detroit operations utilized an outside, "under-running" third-rail. In this format, current was collected by third-rail "shoes" mounted on the locomotive trucks. Since Central's third rail top was covered with wood, the shoes had to press up against the bare underside of the third rail.

S-MOTORS

Central's pioneer electric was experimental motor No. 6000, built by Alco and GE in October 1904. Originally Class L and then Class T-1, it featured a 1-D-1 wheel arrangement. (Electrics use numbers to designate unpowered axles and letters for powered ones, thus a 1-D-1 has four powered axles and guiding pony wheels at either end.) Small rooftop pantographs, situated at each end, were intended for operation within Grand Central Terminal where there might be long gaps in

the third rail as a result of slip-switches or crossovers, and short segments of overhead electrification were positioned to maintain electrical continuity.

Following extensive testing of No. 6000, NYC ordered a fleet of 34 similar electrics, originally Class T-2, built in 1906. Shortly after the beginning of electrified service, a disastrous wreck in the Bronx killed 23 people and injured dozens, compelling the railroad to re-evaluate the tracking ability of its electric motors. The result was that the "T-motors" were rebuilt with two-axle bogey trucks fore and aft which gave them a 2-D-2 wheel arrangement—and supposedly great stability. They were redesignted as S-class motors.

In 1908 and 1909 the railroad ordered 12 more electrics of this upgraded format, Class S-3. In their early years the S-motors were primarily used to power locomotive-hauled train (versus M.U. or self-propelled multiple-unit trains) into Grand Central Terminal. Following the arrival of newer electric locomotives, the S-motors generally were relegated to secondary passenger runs and switching service at Mott Haven Yard and Grand Central. They were the longest-lived of any NYC electric; a few served as Grand Central switchers into the 1980s. The S-motors were a favorite prototype for early toy-train builders, and thousands of miniature "tinplate" S-motor replicas entertained children around the country.

The center-cab S-motors would be a fixture on NYC's Grand Central electrification lines for some 70 years, testamony to the durability of electric locomotives. *The* pioneering S-motor and the only S-1—the 100, built in 1904—switches at Mott Haven coach yard in 1961. *Richard J. Solomon*

"T-MOTORS"

In 1913 Central ordered another type of electric, which assumed the T class (not to be confused with the earlier T motors) and employed an articulated B-B+B-B wheel arrangement, with a platfrom riding on powered trucks ahead of the cab. While significantly lighter than the S-motors, the Ts had an advantage because all of their wheels were powered, thus the full weight of the locomotive was on the drivers. Three classes of T-motors were built, the last arriving in 1926. In their early years, the Ts were dressed in utilitarian black with white lettering and numbers, but in the 1950s some were painted in New York Central's lightning-stripe scheme that had been introduced on the diesel fleet.

Motor 273 is a Class T-3a shown in January 1959 at the Croton-Harmon engine terminal on the Hudson Line. The T-motors' utilitarian look was relieved by NYC's classy lightning-stripe livery. *Richard J. Solomon*

R-2-class motors were built for freight service, but a few had high-speed gearing for passenger assignments, and they were commonly used on mail & express trains operating into New York City on the West Side Freight Line. Several R-2s were sold to interurban Chicago South Shore & South Bend where they could be seen hauling freight well into the 1960s. *E. May, Ed Crist collection*

NEW YORK FREIGHT MOTORS

With the electrification of the West Side Freight Line and other New York-area freight trackage, NYC acquired a fleet of freight motors in addition to the tri-powered box-cabs (see chapter 7). In 1926 the railroad ordered seven steeple-cab electrics with a B-B wheel arrangement, designated Class Q, and a pair of experimental, semi-permanently coupled B-B box-cabs designated Class R followed by 42 six-motor box-cabs in a C-C wheel arrangement, designated R-2. A few of the R-2s were geared for passenger work, and although they were rarely used on passenger trains, they regularly hauled mail and express runs. Interestingly, Central's electric freight operations were largely nocturnal and as a result its freight motors were rarely photographed. Dieselization of the New York freight operations in the late 1940s and early 1950s eliminated the need for specialized freight motors. Some of the R-2s were transfered to the Detroit River Tunnel electrification and a few R-2s were later sold to the Chicago South Shore & South Bend; others remained in the New York area as switchers.

CLEVELAND UNION TERMINAL ELECTRICS

In 1929 and 1930 Alco-GE provided 22 80-foot long 2-C+C-2 electrics for the new Cleveland Union Terminal. These locomotives, Class P-2, were articulated, featured large platforms at either end, and shared a family resemblence with the T-motors. However, they were powered by 3,000-volt d.c. overhead electrication rather than the underrunning third rail found on most NYC electric lines and were lettered for Cleveland Union Terminal. In the early 1950s the electric operations in Cleveland were dieselized, and 21 P-motors were rebuilt for 600-volt third-rail operation on the New York electric lines. The big articulated motors displaced a number of aging T-motors and worked for another 15 years hauling NYC passenger trains out of Grand Central Terminal. A number of them received lightning stripe livery and later the Spartan "cigar band" scheme.

DETROIT RIVER TUNNEL MOTORS

To provide motive power for the Detroit River tunnels on the Michigan Central, NYC ordered a small fleet of 600-volt d.c., third-rail, center-cab electrics. Class R-1, R-1a, and R-1b motors were built between 1910 and 1925; R-1 and R-1b were jointly constructed by Alco and General Electric; the R-1a motors were solely products of GE. In their early years, these R-motors were sublettered for Michigan Central. The advent of dieselization displaced the Detroit River Tunnel electrics, and all were retired by 1956.

Central's Cleveland Union Terminal electrification employed traditional overhead electrification with pantograph collection. The P-class motors that served this electrified district were lettered for Cleveland Union Terminal. *Jay Williams collection*

One of the former Cleveland Union Terminal motors hums along the Harlem River at the Spuyten Duyvil station in 1961. Following their stint on the CUT lines, the P-motors migrated east to New York City where they displaced elderly T-motors. *Richard J. Solomon*

The R-1 class served the Detroit River Tunnel electrification, which included the Detroit passenger depot. This postcard view shows one of the steeple-cab units emerging from one of the twin bores. *David P. Oroszi collection*

99

Against a landscape befitting New York Central's dominance in industrial America, a westbound freight behind a pair of Electro-Motive F-series locomotives are en route through downtown Cleveland in the winter of 1960-1961. First out is a Pacemaker boxcar clad in the eye-catching vermilion and gray that denoted cars assigned to Central's premium *Pacemaker* freight service. Catenary bridges serve as a reminder to NYC's past electric operations through Cleveland Union Terminal. *Hank Goerke*

9

THE FREIGHT SIDE OF NEW YORK CENTRAL

*Pacemaker*s and *Early Bird*s Keep NYC Heartlines Humming

Although the New York Central was and will always be most closely associated with its world-class *20th Century Limited* and its sprawling network of passenger trains, the Central's first and foremost duty was the transport of freight. Firmly entrenched in the heart of industrial America, the NYC moved a tremendous amount of tonnage—even though its fiercest competitor, the Pennsylvania Railroad, served virtually the same market. In later years, the competition became especially severe for Central (and PRR) on account of the relatively short hauls compared to transcons like Santa Fe or "amalgamated transcons" like Burlington-Great Northern. In the post-World War II era, another adversary, the trucking industry, came of age, becoming an ever greater nemesis for NYC than competing railroads.

THE WEST SHORE'S SPECIAL ROLE IN FREIGHT TRAFFIC

The West Shore Line (see chapter 2), may have appeared as a redundant, parallel main line to NYC's highly developed New York City–Buffalo route, but the West Shore served as a very useful freight line. Initially the West Shore was largely a separate operation but was gradually integrated with other NYC routes and became an important part of the system. The most crucial segment was east of Amsterdam, New York, along the southern bank of the Mohawk River and down the west shore of the Hudson. The line was not as busy a passenger route as the Hudson Line, and its comparative dearth of passenger traffic com-bined with superior clearances lent it for development as a freight route. West Shore's terminus in New Jersey also facilitated direct freight connections with several other railroads that terminated in New Jersey across from Manhattan.

Central's lines west of Albany, particularly between Syracuse and Buffalo, were the busiest on the system. Freight and passenger traffic was very heavy, and as late as the early 1950s, NYC was operating more than 100 scheduled trains daily over its Syracuse Division. West of the Albany area, the West Shore ran parallel to the four-track NYC main line, and connections between the two gave NYC operating flexibility; the railroad often detoured trains over the West Shore to avoid congestion. Connections were located at Rotterdam Junction/Hoffmans, Canastota, Kirkville, Bell Isle, Jordan, Lyons, Wayneport, Chili (CHIE-lie) Junction, and at Depew (near Buffalo).

Reliance on the West Shore declined during the mid-1950s. The segment between Lyons and Rotterdam saw very little through traffic after 1952, and although the West Shore route remained intact until 1957, it was gradually abandoned in sections west of Rotterdam Junction/Hoffmans (just west of Schenectady). NYC retained portions of the West Shore to serve local industries and as main-line bypass routes, such as the stretch between Wayneport and Chili Junction which served as a bypass around Rochester. East of Rotterdam Junction, the West Shore main line became a primary freight route between the

Train BH-2 (Buffalo–Corning, New York) is eastbound on the old New York, West Shore & Buffalo main line east of Newark, New York. Central used its West Shore trackage, which paralleled the Water Level Route main line between New York and Buffalo, as a relief valve for traffic on the busy NYC main line, visible in the background in this scene from the mid-1950s. *NYC, Tim Doherty collection*

Capital District (Albany and environs) and New York City. In the 1950s the West Shore might typically handle four or five scheduled freights each direction daily between Selkirk and Weehawken.

FAST FREIGHT

Traditional American rail freight operations were notoriously slow. A car could take several days to move just a few hundred miles and might spend much of its time languishing in yards. Yet, before the advent of motorized trucking and paved roads, even glacially slow freights were faster than the alternatives. However, by the 1920s improved highway transportation was forcing railroads to accelerate freight schedules and offer better service. Less-than-carload (LCL) business, which typically consisted of shipments smaller than what would fill a standard boxcar, was most affected because door-to-door truck service proved more competitive than existing rail service.

In the early 1930s, the Cotton Belt introduced its highly successful *Blue Streak Merchandise* specifically designed to recapture LCL business by offering prompt, scheduled service at low rates. In like manner during 1934, Central inaugurated fast *Merchandiser* trains to carry perishable (produce, meats, and fruits) and LCL traffic between New York City and Buffalo. Rather than ambling freight trains toting cars with widely varied destinations both on and off line, the *Merchandiser*s were dedicated through trains that operated at speeds up to 65 miles per hour—much faster than the railroad's typical drag freights of the period. The *Merchandiser*s met with considerable success, but were discontinued in 1942 as a result of wartime restrictions.

In May 1946, the railroad reintroduced the concept with the inauguration of its *Pacemaker* service. Named for Central's high-speed, all-coach New York–Chicago *Pacemaker* passenger train, this service was a skillfully planned marketing strategy aimed at recapturing LCL traffic. Railroad advertising emphasized the *Pacemaker* as fast express service with dedicated through trains that did not require rehandling or switching. According to ads, the *Pacemaker* was a day faster than previous services. When introduced, *Pacemaker* freights operated between Manhattan and Buffalo/ Niagara Falls on a 11-hour schedule, including pickup stops at Albany, Utica, De Witt (Syracuse), and Rochester. Carrying the symbol NB-1 (New York–Buffalo), the *Pacemaker* departed Manhattan at 7:45 P.M. and arrived at Buffalo 6:50 A.M. the following morning. Later, an hour was cut from the schedule.

Initially, *Pacemaker* trains featured distinctive, assigned equipment. Specially designed boxcars built for the service sported a flashy vermilion-and-gray livery with "Pacemaker" written on the sides in script. To provide a significantly smoother ride at speed and reduce incidents of in-transit damage, *Pacemaker* cars were equipped with high-speed trucks that used stabilizers and bolsters to minimize lateral and vertical motion, and rubber-cushioned couplers to retard slack action. A fleet of 425 cars were built by Despatch Shops, and as service expanded, the fleet grew to 1,000. Later, older cars were added to *Pacemaker* service and painted accordingly. Although *Pacemaker* cars were usually used for this service, it was not an exclusive arrangement, and common boxcars often would be assigned to *Pacemaker* trains. The service included free pick up and delivery using NYC-owned trucks.

In early years of service, the *Pacemaker*s were assigned modern L-3 and L-4 Mohawks and S-class Niagaras west of the electrified lines, but these priority trains were among the first road freights to regularly receive diesel power and were largely dieselized after 1948. Typically, *Pacemaker* trains would leave Manhattan with 25 cars and make pickups along the way, handling some 50 cars into Buffalo; trains could carry as many as 75 cars. On the four-track main, the *Pacemaker* used the two tracks normally assigned to passenger trains and operated at a top speed of 65 mph.

Pacemaker service was gradually expanded. In April 1949, a pair of dedicated Boston–Buffalo trains were added, and later that year service was extended west of Buffalo to Cleveland. By 1950 *Pacemaker* service reached most Midwestern cities within Central's service region. *Pacemaker* service survived into the mid-1950s, although it was de-emphasized following the 1954 introduction of the *Early Bird* trains.

Whereas *Pacemaker* was aimed at LCL traffic, Central's *Early Bird* service was a marketing ploy aimed at recapturing carload traffic

With the mercury nearing 100, an eastbound frreight carrying a block of stockcars eases past the penstock and water plug at Rome, New York, as the head brakeman operates the "shower," flushing upper and lower decks in each car and cooling the hogs. The refrigerator cars behind the stock block portends the fate of the livestock. *NYC, Mike Del Vecchio collection*

Creating its own dark storm clouds, Mohawk 3123 hustles freight along the four-track Water Level Route main line near Rome circa 1950. *H. W. Pontin, Mike Del Vecchio collection*

"The long reach of Pacemaker service" is outlined in a handy brochure distributed by the Central. Included were service descriptions and schedules. *C. W. Newton collection*

through improved scheduling. In 1950, NYC had roughly 100 scheduled fast freights systemwide, including *Pacemaker*s. *Early Bird* advertising promoted a network of even faster, tightly scheduled through freights. New York–Chicago service was promised in just 29 hours, "on time one day earlier" than previous trains. Dozens of *Early Bird* trains were scheduled to link most major cities in the New York Central System. A cartoon bird, dressed in an engineer's cap and carrying a railroad pocket watch, was featured in advertising. However,

although some boxcars were painted with *Early Bird* advertising, this service was not as distinct as the *Pacemaker*.

The trains hauled everything from aluminum sheets to flasks of wine, and an ad from 1955 lists more than 50 different commodities shipped on *Early Bird* trains. The service was fairly short-lived. By the late 1950s, Central was focusing promotion efforts on its new intermodal concept, the Flexi-Van, a hybrid design of today's freight container and TOFC (trailer-on-flatcar) equipment.

This clever bit of marketing from Central's Flexi-Van era incorporated slide-rule technology to inform shippers of scheduled departures and arrivals through Central's principal connections. *C. W. Newton*

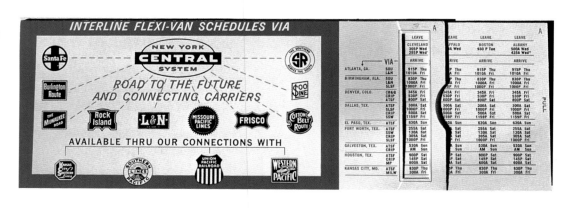

FLEXI-VAN

One problem with traditional TOFC service is that the highway wheels must be taken along as parasitic tare; further, the wheels result in a flatcar load of excessive height. Loading and unloading TOFC flatcars, usually circus-style back then, was slow, labor intensive, and cumbersome. NYC introduced a distinctive container technology, dubbed Flexi-Van, that addressed these problems.

In 1957, Strick Division of Fruehauf Corporation developed an experimental flatcar equipped with a small motor-driven turntable. A container could be loaded on the flatcar by backing up the truck trailer at right angles to the car and sliding the container off the highway bogie onto the turntable. Then the container could then be rotated and locked into place on the car. Unloading involved the procedure in reverse. Flexi-Van possessed the advantages of: (1) low van tare (no running gear); (2) lower center of gravity; (3) reduced wind resistance; (4) random access to the containers at terminals; and (5) low clearance requirements for NYC routes into Boston and New York City. Central ordered production cars with two turntables per car, each car capable of handling two 40-foot vans. Ultimately, NYC bought over 7,000 vans and 859 Flexi-Van flatcars, equipping the railroad to run 50 daily high-speed Flexi-Van trains, dubbed *SuperVan* trains.

Unfortunately, few other roads embraced the technology (Milwaukee Road and Illinois Central were two exceptions), and Flexi-van thus became a largely NYC-only captive phenomenon. The need to interchange intermodal traffic became overwhelming, and in 1964 NYC bought into the TrailerTrain consortium to assure a supply of conventional trailers. Gradually, the Flexi-Van technology faded into oblivion, replaced by the more familiar trailer-on-flat-car piggyback. But the boom in container traffic during the 1980s and 1990s prove that NYC was ahead of its time.

AUTOMOTIVE TRAFFIC

New York Central and the Pennsylvania Railroad competed fiercely for lucrative auto traffic. Ironically, NYC, who's extensive passenger service was decimated by the growth in highway transportation, benefited greatly from the growth of auto-industry freight traffic and for many years claimed the title as the world's

NYC's Milk Train Era

An NYC milk train nears Kingston, New York, in 1947 on the line once belonging to the Ulster & Delaware branch. *C. W. Jernstrom, collection of Herbert H. Harwood Jr.*

New York City, one of the largest consumers of dairy products in the United States, enjoyed one of the most developed milk-train networks in the nation. As late as the 1940s, New York Central delivered more than 40 percent of the city's dairy products, representing roughly 1 million gallons of milk daily. New York's "Milk Shed" (dairy-producing region) extended across Upstate New York and encompassed parts of Vermont, Massachusetts, Connecticut, New Jersey, and Pennsylvania.

The challenge of transporting milk involved gathering fresh milk from a wide production area, keeping it cool en route to market, and getting it there expeditiously. In the transport of dairy products, hours mattered; conventional freight trains would not provide sufficiently fast service for dairy products. Central developed a carefully scheduled network of trains that gathered and delivered milk on a daily basis.

Early in the twentieth century, milk was typically transported in 10-gallon metal canisters and cases of glass bottles in insulated refrigerated boxcars. Gradually, specially designed insulated tank cars replaced conventional can-carrying cars. By World War II, the railroad was moving roughly 75 percent of its milk in insulated tank cars.

Every morning in the Milk Shed region, local passenger trains of the NYC, Rutland, and other carriers collected fresh milk from farms along the route. Although these trains operated at a more relaxed pace than the railroad's intercity limiteds, they maintained a strict schedule, expediting milk and passengers as quickly as possible. These trains deposited their milk cars at central locations where they were reassembled into solid milk trains for delivery to New York City. These through runs made their way down the Hudson, Harlem, and West Shore lines beginning in the early evening and arrived for delivery in New York City late at night or early in the morning, moving milk from cow to consumer in as little as 24 hours.

In the 1940s an average of three solid milk trains per day terminated in Manhattan; milk cars were also dropped at Spuyten Duyvil in the Bronx. A fourth solid milk train, carrying milk produced in the Catskill region, terminated a Weehawken. The solid milk trains were usually handled by NYC's fastest freight locomotives, such as a Mohawk. By the mid-1950s, competition from over-the-road trucks seriously cut into milk-train operation throughout the country, including that of NYC. By the 1960s, the era of the milk run had passed into history.

Central's Manhattan yards reflected the diversity of commerce within New York. The 33rd Street yards handled perishable traffic and was normally filled with orange and yellow refrigerator cars that had carried fruits and vegetables from the West Coast. *Jim Shaughnessy, Mike Del Vecchio collection*

leading transporter of new automobiles. During the 1960s the number of new vehicles carried by the railroad increased dramatically. In 1962, the railroad moved approximately 500,000 new cars; in 1965, Central carried nearly 1.2 million cars, representing roughly 12 percent of American new car production.

Until the late 1950s, autos shipped by rail were transported in special boxcars—an inefficient and cumbersome way to ship new vehicles, making railroads easy prey to the trucking industry. The introduction of the bi- and tri-level auto-rack in the late 1950s changed all that. A single train of tri-level auto-racks could carry as many 2,300 new cars and significantly lowered transportation costs, not only for auto manufacturers but for railroads. Auto traffic resurged on America's railroads.

The value of auto traffic was reflected in NYC's freight schedules. In the mid-1960s, one of the highest priority trains on the system was the exclusive auto-carrying "multi-level" freight, ML-12, which departed Detroit eastbound every day for Selkirk Yard (Albany) via Toledo and Cleveland. Carrying up to 150 auto-racks—each carrying as many as 15 autos—ML-12 was typically assigned eight high-horsepower locomotives and was permitted 70 miles per hour on the main line. At Selkirk, the auto-racks were redistributed to other trains while some cars were unloaded and trucked to final nearby destinations.

METROPOLITAN NEW YORK FREIGHT FACILITIES

New York's passenger terminals are world famous, but its freight terminals are almost enitrely unknown, even to most city residents. NYC's *20th Century Limited* remains one of the nation's most remembered passenger trains, but the railroad's numerous freight trains that supplied New York with its daily needs went unheeded and largely unseen.

Since the mid-1800s, New York was the largest metropolitan area in the United States. The city's unusual geographic position and extreme congestion caused by the vast numbers of people living in a comparatively compact region made freight delivery particularly challenging. John A. Droege in his book *Freight Terminals and Trains* described New York City as the most complicated freight terminal in the world. Most of New York City is located on islands in New York Harbor, and although more than a dozen railroads served New York, only NYC had a direct surface rail line to Manhattan—New York's primary business district and the heart of many industries. Other rail lines could only reach New York by way of car floats or highway transportation, giving NYC a great advantage in the New York market.

For many years NYC was the largest freight-hauler serving the city, and New York was among the railroad's largest single freight destinations. In 1920 Central moved nearly 114 million tons of freight into New York, and by the end of World War II this figure had jumped to nearly 181 million tons. By 1960, despite an ongoing loss of business to highway traffic, NYC still moved more than 133 million tons of freight to New York City.

Central's West Side Freight Line was in fact the old Hudson River Railroad main line into the city. By 1900 this route had become known as the West Side line and was a largely double-track artery that followed the shore of the Hudson River on the west side of Manhattan Island. In later years, principal yards were located at 60th Street and 33rd Street, with smaller yards and terminals at 145th Street, 41st Street, 17th Street, and at St. Johns Park near Chambers Street, end of the line.

The West Side route became increasingly congested as traffic swelled to accommodate the growing city. By the mid-1920s it was accommodating an average of 1,700 cars every day. Complicating operational problems south of the yards at 33rd Street was street trackage on 11th Avenue that continued south to St. Johns Park. For this street service Central maintained a fleet of shrouded "steam dummies"—steam locomotives shrouded to hide moving parts in an effort to placate Victorian-era aesthetic sensibilities and concerns that locomotives would frighten horses. Furthermore the city required a flagman on horseback to lead all trains through the street to warn pedestrians and motorists. The vast scope of NYC's Manhattan operations required an army of urban cowboys patroling in front of its street-bound freight trains.

Such operational difficulties led the railroad

and the city to investigate alternatives. During World War I, a six-track tunnel was considered for lower Manhattan, two tracks to serve freight operations and the remainder for a rapid-transit line. Ultimately, Central decided instead to elevate its tracks south of 34th, resulting in one of the most unique freight railways in North America. Work on the project began in the late 1920s, and the line opened in 1934. Elevated on a double-track concrete viaduct, the rebuilt line passed directly *through* numerous factories and warehouses. Many businesses had sidings inside their buildings, and some companies had elevators to move cars up and down within the buildings! Most of the route was electrified with NYC's under-running 600-volt third rail. The line relocation also included some strategic yard expansion. On its completion, Central's Manhattan yards had a 4,800-car capacity.

Although the West Side Line moved a considerable amount of freight into New York City, NYC also operated the largest railroad marine fleet in New York Harbor. In 1912 this included 21 steam tugs and 49 car floats which handled an average of 760 cars a day. By 1930 the railroad had 29 tugs and 66 car floats, but by 1964 the fleet had diminished to only 11 tugs and 22 car floats.

On the Jersey shore at Weehawken, Central operated its largest marine terminal, served by its West Shore line. This complex facility featured a large brick grain elevator, a fair-sized

NYC had the largest marine fleet of any railroad serving Manhattan Island. Here several NYC tugboats await call to duty at the Weehawken piers in the summer of 1964. *Richard J. Solomon*

107

At the "Hump" N. Y. C. R. R. Yards, East Syracuse, N. Y.

Although sometimes regarded as a modern innovation, hump yards date from early in the twentieth century as this postcard scene of East Syracuse (De Witt) yard depicts. *Mike Schafer collection*

yard, and numerous docks. From here, cars and freight were floated across the Hudson to a variety of terminals in New York City, including 60th Street yard, 37th Street station, and piers at West 42nd Street and Barclay Street on the Hudson side, and Pier 34 on the east side of Manhattan along the East River.

YARD COMPLEXES ACROSS THE SYSTEM

In the late era, NYC developed a network of super yards that handled the majority of the railroad's classification work. Some of these yards had roots to the turn of the century, while others were purely modern-era innovations. Many were conventional "flat-switching" yards in which cars were sorted by switchers onto their appropriate tracks. By the 1960s New York Central, like many other railroads, also operated several "hump" yards in which cars were sorted through gravity. Strings of freight cars to be sorted are slowly pushed up and over an artificial hill; the cars are uncoupled and allowed to coast down into their appropriate yard track, with either remote-controlled or automatic retarders slowing them down along the way.

The Central had hundreds of yards throughout its system, from large classification yards to countless small storage and staging yards for nearby industries. A roundup of the notable facilities follows:

Boston & Albany: B&A's large Beacon Park Yard, located three miles west of South Station, served the Boston area. The railroad's other major yards were located Worcester and West Springfield—the latter also the location of B&A's locomotive shops.

Capital District: Selkirk Yard, opened in 1924 in conjunction with the Castleton Cutoff (Chapter 3), largely supplanted Central's sprawling West Albany yards which had served as the primary freight marshaling point for the Albany/Troy/Schenectady area since the 1850s. Prior to Selkirk, West Albany was comprised of 73 miles of trackage and had capacity for 6,100 cars, putting it among the largest yards on the NYC. It also featured an important shop complex. Though less strategic after Selkirk opened, West Albany survived as a gathering point for local traffic.

Selkirk was (and is) an enormous facility, six miles long, built near the site of an old West Shore yard and named for a nearby village. It incorporated a hump yard and classified traffic moving over the Mohawk Division, West Shore, Hudson Line, and the B&A. Selkirk was modernized in the mid-1960s as a large, computerized "push-button" hump facility and dedicated as Alfred E. Perlman Yard. In 1966 it had a capacity of 5,195 cars.

Central New York: Utica, 95 miles west of Albany and a junction point with lines to the North Country, featured a three-mile-long flat switching yard which in the 1940s served as NYC's largest transfer facility.

Built in 1904, De Witt Yard east of Syracuse was among the oldest hump yards on the Central and featured two humps to accommodate both east- and westbound traffic. The westbound hump had a 4,980-car capacity while the eastbound held 5,855 cars. For many years it was one of the largest, busiest yards in the U.S. The hump was worked by 0-8-8-0 Mallets compounds until the mid-1940s.

In the diesel era, De Witt was the location of

a primary diesel shop and the base for most Alco and General Electric locomotives. Bell Isle Yard, west of Syracuse, was an older facility that primarily served the West Shore. Central maintained a small yard on the Water Level Route main line at Lyons, New York, for traffic to and from the lines down into Pennsylvania.

In the steam era, Wayneport, between Lyons and Rochester, featured an extensive servicing facility where locomotives could be replenished with water, coal, and sand right on the main line to minimize delays. A few miles farther west at East Rochester was Despatch Shops where an NYC subsidiary manufactured refrigerator cars and other freight equipment. Rochester's primary yard was located on the east side of town at Goodman Street.

Buffalo/Niagara Falls: Buffalo was among one of the most complex railroad terminals on the NYC between New York and Chicago. Here Central crossed and interchanged with numerous other railroads and served dozens of major industries. In 1956 the railroad built Frontier Yard east of downtown Buffalo. As Central's first large electronically controlled hump yard, Frontier was designed to supplant eight older facilities, including the vast Gardenville Yard, Buffalo's older hump on the city's south side. Despite Frontier's 5,140-car capacity, the scope of Buffalo-area operations required that NYC maintain several fair-sized flat-switching yards in the area to serve local industries. At Niagara Falls, a large, flat yard accommodated chemical and interchange traffic moving through the Niagara Gateway.

Pittsburgh and Youngstown: NYC affiliate Pittsburgh & Lake Erie operated a large yard and shops at McKees Rocks near Pittsburgh. In May 1958 the railroad opened Gateway Yard at Youngstown, Ohio, replacing several smaller yards in that area. This immense facility was five miles long and covered roughly 200 acres. Gateway's 35-track hump classification yard had a capacity for 1,697 cars while its 21-track receiving yard had a 3,076-car capacity. Gateway could process up to 2,700 cars a day.

Cleveland: The railroad's primary Cleveland-area facility was Collinwood Yard which featured a large, flat switching yard and the railroad's primary shops for Electro-Motive diesels. Iron ore off Great Lakes boats and destined for NYC trains passed through boat-to-

Heartbeat of Central's Midwestern freight operations was Collinwood Yard on Cleveland's east side. Here, freight was sorted for the New York–Chicago main line, the Columbus/Cincinnati line, the St. Louis line, and the route down to Pittsburgh. On August 15, 1964, three cab units (two Electro-Motive diesels and a Fairbanks-Morse locomotive) are eastbound at Collinwood. Steam had been gone for several years, but Collinwood's landmark coaling tower still stood. *Dave Ingles, Mike Schafer collection*

Toting a wooden caboose, Electro-Motive NW2 switcher 9504 (formerly belonging to New York, Ontario & Western, abandoned in 1957) putts about Air Line Yard on Toledo's west side on a summer day in 1962. *Hank Goerke*

Central moved a substantial amount of freight—mostly ore and coal—through the huge dock complex at Ashtabula, Ohio. *David P. Oroszi collection*

train transfer facilities at Cleveland's harbor on Lake Erie.

Toledo: Toledo had two main yards. Air Line Yard, a flat-switched facility, was located west of the passenger depot on the Water Level Route main line. Stanley Yard, on the old Toledo & Ohio Central southeast of downtown, featured a large hump with a 42-track classification yard that could hold 5,090 cars. The enormous Toledo docks through which NYC received iron ore were shared with the Baltimore & Ohio.

Columbus: West Columbus yard, built on a Toledo & Ohio Central alignment, was a substantial facility in this Big Four hub city. It was a flat-switched yard used by trains off all Big Four and T&OC lines entering the city. The yard was abandoned by Penn Central, which built a new facility—Buckeye Yard—elsewhere in the city.

Cincinnati: Sharon Yard was the primary Cincinnati-area yard, featuring a hump that was built in 1908. The yard was converted from a "rider" hump (in which brakemen rode with cars down the hump to slow them with the car's manual brakes) to a a double-retarder hump in 1928. In the modern era Sharon had a capacity for 3,830 cars.

Detroit: Detroit-area freight operations were closely linked to the automobile industry and grew enormously as the auto-industry flourished. Junction Yard in West Detroit was Central's primary yard in the region, serving as a hub for numerous smaller yards in the Detroit/Windsor (Ontario) area including North Yard, Mount Road Yard, Huber Yard, and River Rouge Yard. Junction featured a traditional hump with 32 classification tracks and a capacity for 5,529 cars.

Elkhart: In the modern era, NYC built two large computer-controlled hump yards in Indiana, one on the Chicago main line at Elkhart and the other on the Big Four near Indianapolis. These modern yards supplanted a host of older facilities, streamlined Central's freight operations at the west end of system, and simplified interchange with other lines. Elkhart Yard was built on the site an older facility in 1957 and dedicated to Robert R. Young. Elkhart featured a modern electronic hump with 72 classification tracks, and the whole facility could hold nearly 7,000 cars. It primarily handled traffic moving via the Chicago gateway and classified interchange traffic to many Chicago-area roads. On most days it processed roughly 30 inbound trains and built a like number of outbounds, making it one of NYC's busiest yards in the 1960s.

Indianapolis: Serving Indiana's largest city, Avon Yard—also known as Big Four Yard—was built in 1960 as a modern hump facility. It featured 53 classification tracks, a 7-track departure yard, and 9-track receiving yard. Avon's primary function was to classify interchange traffic moving to, from, and through the St. Louis gateway. Avon pre-blocked cars for the Missouri Pacific, Frisco, Cotton Belt, and other St. Louis connections. Avon also processed traffic for the Cincinnati–Chicago line and the Terra Haute–Evansville line. The yard originated more than 20 symbol freights daily to points all around the system.

Chicagoland: Central's primary facility in the Chicago area was a vast complex known as Gibson Yard, at Hammond, Indiana. Actually comprising several sub-yards, Gibson was shared with subsidiary Indiana Harbor Belt, which distributed traffic off of Central's ex-Michigan Central and ex-LS&MS lines to on-line (IHB) industries as well as the yards of other railroads belting Chicago's south and west sides. A relatively small NYC yard at Englewood (63rd Street) on Chicago's South Side served Chicago proper (in the Conrail era, it was a piggyback yard), and an an ex-MC yard at Kensington (115th Street) was also used by Illinois Central and Chicago South Shore & South Bend. In addition to the IHB, the NYC-controlled Chicago River & Indiana Railroad helped distribute traffic to South Side industries.

Central's main freight facility serving metro Chicago was Gibson Yard at Hammond, Indiana. Although many freights terminated and originated at Gibson, NYC often operated selected freights through Gibson direct to the yards of connecting carriers via NYC subsidiary Indiana Harbor Belt. In the summer of 1967, a new General Electric locomotive teams with two older Electro-Motive cab units bound for Gibson yard with an eastbound freight out of IHB's Blue Island yard. *Mike Schafer*

Oh what Fun it is to ride—
...on a New York Central train!

It's **Fun to join** in the holiday good fellowship on New York Central's luxurious new observation or lounge cars . . . many of them for coach passengers, too.

It's **Fun to order** yourself a piping hot meal in New York Central's new streamlined dining cars . . . and enjoy every course with a big helping of scenery on the side!

It's **Fun to snuggle down** for a winter's nap in Central's comfortable sleeping car berths or private rooms . . . with never a care for the weather out there, as you sleep the miles away!

It's **Fun to relax** in a lean-back seat on Central's new fleet of cozily air-conditioned coaches . . . and watch the winter world roll past your wide, sightseeing window.

Yes, it's fun to enjoy the NEW in

THIS IS AN ALL WEATHER MAP!

Winter or summer, storm or fair, New York Central's new daylight streamliners and overnight "Dreamliners" get you there in comfort . . . via this dependable 11,000-mile network.

NEW NEW YORK CENTRAL
The Water Level Route—You Can Sleep

NEW YORK CENTRAL SYSTEM

Inviting magazine ads such as this memorable Christmas-themed promotion were the hallmark of Central's postwar introduction of new streamliners and "Dreamliners." Such idealism would, unfortunately, be short-lived. *Mike Schafer collection*

PASSENGER TRAINS OF THE NEW YORK CENTRAL

From Flange-Wheeled Stagecoaches to the Great Steel Fleet

From all the press that it has received, one might think that the *20th Century Limited*—one of the most famous trains in the world and the subject of numerous magazine articles, Broadway plays, and books—was the only passenger train ever operated by the New York Central. Fact was, the New York Central System blanketed two of the most heavily populated and industrialized regions of the United States—the Northeast and Upper Midwest—and in serving (and linking) those regions operated a passenger-train network of amazing variety and scope.

It all officially started on August 9, 1831, when the first Mohawk & Hudson passenger train lurched into history on its maiden voyage between Albany and Schenectady. As each railroad in the chain of lines destined to make up the first New York Central Railroad, between Albany and Buffalo, was completed, each began operating their own passenger trains. Around 1841, through-car passenger service was established between the two cities, and on June 4, 1853, a special excursion train operated through from Albany to Niagara Falls to celebrate the impending consolidation that would form the New York Central Railroad. Through passenger trains between Albany and Buffalo/Niagara Falls would become the rule, not the exception.

Meanwhile, the Hudson River Railroad had opened in 1851 and shortly after, six trains were operating each way between New York and Albany, with connections at the latter for NYC trains to and from Buffalo. Travel between New York and Buffalo could be done in 18 hours. In 1858, sleeping-car service was established by T. T. Woodruff & Company (as the New York Central Sleeping Car Company) between Albany and Buffalo.

Unfortunately, direct connection between New York–Albany, Boston–Albany, and Albany–Buffalo trains did not exist until the first bridge was completed across the Hudson River in 1866. Following this momentous event, the Central's famous "Red Trains" were inaugurated between New York City and Buffalo. Painted a flashy crimson rather than the conventional yellow of trains of that period, the new flyers carried improved Wagner sleeping cars.

We need not complete the merger histories that advanced from this point—that's been covered in the first two chapters of this book—but the story was much the same with any new railroad absorbed into the New York Central System family: the component railroad's passenger services were integrated into the overall system following merger—if they hadn't been already. Over time, the haphazard passenger-train schedules of the individual railroads were consolidated or refined to operate more as a network. For example, Wagner sleeping cars were instituted between New York and Cincinnati once the Big Four lines had come under the Central umbrella.

Meanwhile, George M. Pullman's company had also entered the sleeping-car business and was operating sleepers on the Lake Shore & Michigan Southern and Michigan Central between Chicago and Buffalo. In 1866 Pullman introduced "hotel cars" on the

MC—luxury cars equipped with berths and—a new novelty—dining service, supposedly the first on any American railroad. Alas, the Vanderbilts held a strong financial interest in the Wagner Car Company and eventually Pullman's cars were shut out from operation on NYC&HR-controlled lines.

By the early 1870s the NYC owned nearly 600 passenger cars. The railroad was well entrenched in New York City—the first Grand Central opened in 1871—and the Lake Shore & Michigan Southern had just come into the NYC fold. The LS&MS was a critical addition to the NYC, and now New York–Chicago coordinated service was in the offing. Rival Pennsylvania Railroad was also in the final stages of completing its New York–Chicago lines, so the impetus was there for Central to look at the big picture for what would be its premier passenger route: New York–Chicago.

Central's Water Level Route all the way to Chicago and four-track main line across New York and part of Ohio was the perfect foundation for high-speed passenger-train service, and on July 4, 1875, the first of a generation of New York–Chicago flyers entered service, supplementing existing conventional trains on the route. Departing New York in the wee hours on

Sundays only, the limited-stop train—which reached speeds of 75 miles per hour—was scheduled into Chicago at 8 A.M. on Mondays.

Later in the 1800s, George H. Daniels became Central's passenger agent—and the person who almost single-handedly vaulted NYC to world-class status in the realm of passenger trains. In 1891 Daniels launched the *Empire State Express,* a new high-speed day train between New York and Buffalo designed to supplement the *Chicago Limited,* which was burdened with considerable intrastate traffic in New York State. On May 10, 1893, the *Empire State Express,* in the charge of NYC&HR's famed 4-4-0 No. 999, reached a purported speed of 112.5 miles per hour. Well over 100 years later, the *Empire State Express* still served the New York–Buffalo market. Also in 1893 and in recognition of the Columbian Exposition in Chicago, Daniels launched yet another express, the *Exposition Flyer.* The *Flyer* made the 960-plus-mile trip in an amazing 20 hours.

Although these and other Central trains had been equipped with Wagner sleeping cars, by the turn of the century Vanderbilts' control of the Wagner Car Company had slipped such that the Pullman Company was able to absorb

Wagner. Undoubtedly, George M. Pullman must have taken great delight in seeing his sleeping cars become commonplace on NYC trains—and they would remain so until the end of the 1950s.

Daniels best-known innovation became what many historians feel was the world's most famous train. When inaugurated on June 2, 1902 (the same day that adversary Pennsylvania Railroad launched its *Pennsylvania Special*, later renamed *Broad Way Limited*), the all-Pullman, all-electric-lighted *20th Century* boasted a barber shop, valet, stenographer, and maid service. The end-to-end running time of the five-car train (three sleepers, buffet-lounge, diner) matched that of the *Exposition Flyer*, but in 1905 when the *20th Century Limited* (the "Limited" having been added when the train's schedule was restructured with limited stops) was upgraded with newer equipment, the timing was reduced to 18 hours. In 1909, a Boston section was added. The *Century* was marketed to the very wealthy, while the masses were consigned to trains of lesser status on the route, such as the *Lake Shore Limited*.

As the New York Central System matured into a powerful enterprise during the early twentieth century, its vast network of routes was teeming with passenger trains offering all levels of service. Its showcase route would always be New York–Chicago (with two different routings between Buffalo and Chicago, via southern Ontario or through Ohio), fed by traffic to and from Boston. However, service between Boston/New York and St. Louis—the western extremity of NYC passenger service—via Cleveland and Indianapolis was also significant as was service to Cincinnati via Cleveland and Columbus, Ohio.

THE STREAMLINER ERA

Like nearly all other U.S. railroads, the Central's passenger revenues began to be eroded by the automobile during the 1920s. However, the Depression that followed the Crash of '29 dealt a particularly severe blow by drastically curtailing Americans' ability for discretionary travel. As revenues plummeted, railroads searched for ways to woo passengers back to the rails, or to at least reduce operating costs on routes most severely affected. For example, Central in 1933 introduced its Composite Passenger Service Program, aimed at reducing duplicative services by coordinating efforts with competing railroads who were in the same dire straits. For example, Central sought to consolidate Detroit–Pittsburgh operations with rival Pennsylvania.

Shortly after arrival from New York on September 2, 1931, the *20th Century Limited* shares the platforms and huge arch train shed of Chicago's La Salle Street Station with a conveyance of considerably less stature—the Rock Island suburban train at right. *Cal's Classics*

Gilded by the setting sun, the Chicago-bound *20th Century Limited* struts its new Dreyfuss-designed streamlined equipment along the Hudson River circa 1938. As an art form, the distinctive profile of the Dreyfuss Hudson would long outlive the *Century*, the New York Central Railroad, and the locomotives themselves. *Jay Williams collection*

The answer came in 1934 in the form of two little experimental trains that had been built, one for the Union Pacific (the M-10000) and one for the Chicago, Burlington & Quincy (*Zephyr* 9900). They were lightweight trains powered by internal combustion engines, and they were known as "streamliners." The trains were wildly successful and they inspired other railroads to embark on streamlining programs for their passenger services.

George Daniels was long gone by this time, or he probably would have immediately put NYC on the streamliner bandwagon. But the Depression-era Central was a conservative company, and it entered the streamliner movement cautiously and on its own terms. Rather than purchase streamlined equipment

new and risk dealing with new fangled diesel power, NYC built its first streamliner from surplus suburban coaches built in the 1920s and powered it with a steam locomotive. Work was done by Big Four's Beech Grove Shops near Indianapolis and West Albany Shops, with styling handled by industrial designer Henry Dreyfus, and on June 25, 1936, New York Central unveiled its *Mercury* streamliner. The train entered high-speed day service between Cleveland and Detroit. An instant hit, *Mercury* service was soon upgraded and expanded, and the stage was set for NYC to introduce one of the world's greatest streamliners.

The 1938 streamlining of NYC's *20th Century Limited* and adversary Pennsylvania's New York–Chicago *Broadway Limited* brought

those two flagships to the pinnacles of their paralleling careers. Oddly, the project was behind the scenes a joint effort of NYC, PRR, the Pullman Company, and Pullman-Standard. The cars for both trains were ordered as a group for cost-saving reasons, but interior arrangements and design differed vastly since each railroad had hired separate designers.

Again, Central hired Dreyfuss who rendered this latest edition of the *Century* stunning, sophisticated, and stylish beyond anything that had been done to date on any railroad. The 1938 *Century* was a train without peer, from its rakish streamlined Hudson to its mid-train double diners (transformed after dinner into "Café Century," an elegant night club with piped-in music) to its stellar, city-themed observation-lounge cars.

Sixty-two cars were ordered, enough for four *Century* trainsets (the train often operated in multiple sections to accommodate demand; meanwhile PRR's *Broadway* suffered from lack of patrons) as well as to update sleeper service on the *Century*'s haute running mate, the **Commodore Vanderbilt**, and on the New York–St. Louis *Southwestern Limited*.

Following the *Century*, the next two "new" streamliners were again homebuilt jobs, introduced in 1939. The *Chicago Mercury* brought

The *Mercury* was NYC's frugal but successful entry into streamlining. Surplus 1920s-era commuter cars served as the foundation for the trains, one of which is shown in Detroit–Cincinnati service near Dayton, Ohio, in the 1950s. *Alvin Schultze*

★ ADVANCED ★ ENGINEERING

BEHIND EVERY PASSENGER CAR CREATION

Prior to World War II, Central placed orders for light-weight rolling stock with a number of builders, including Pressed Steel Car Company of Pittsburgh. A 1943 brochure issued by the firm featured one of the 25 PSC coaches delivered in 1942. *Mike Schafer collection*

THE PRESSED STEEL CAR COMPANY, the pioneer builders of steel passenger cars, has been building passenger equipment for over forty years. The two deluxe coaches illustrated on these pages are outstanding examples of modern construction in recent years.

PRESSED STEEL
CAR COMPANY, INC.
PITTSBURGH, PA.

An A-B set of Electro-Motive E7-series diesels wearing Central's short-lived light gray scheme rolls a newly equipped *Ohio State Limited* through Moraine, Ohio, on the Fourth of July 1948. *R. D. Acton Sr.*

streamliner service to the Chicago–Detroit market while the high-speed, all-coach New York–Chicago *Pacemaker*—initially a reconditioned heavyweight train, then equipped with modernized heavyweight cars—brought luxury overnight coach service to passengers traveling between those two cities. Next was the *James Whitcomb Riley* between Chicago and Cincinnati, re-equipped 1941 with a combination of new streamlined cars and modernized heavyweight cars. Later that year, the *Empire State Express* was completely streamlined with all-new cars and a streamstyled Pacific . . . on a date set in infamy: December 7, 1941. Despite

much advance publicity, the headlines for the new *ESE* were much overshadowed by Pearl Harbor and America's entry into World War II.

Streamlining had spread fast on the Central. In addition to those trains which had been entirely streamlined, many new lightweight cars had by 1941 been delivered for "general service," to be mixed with heavyweight rolling stock on several Chicago–New York trains (including the *Wolverine, Lake Shore Limited, Fifth Avenue Special, Iroquois, Water Level Limited, Forest City*), on the Boston–Chicago *New England States*, on the New York–St. Louis *Knickerbocker*, the New York–Cincinnati *Ohio State Limited*, the New York–Detroit *Detroiter*, the New York–Syracuse *Genesee*, the New York–Cleveland *Cleveland Limited*, and other runs. The result of Central's aggressive upgrading with streamlined equipment was dubbed "The Great Steel Fleet," mirroring NYC's powerful presence in the most industrialized corner of the U.S.

At the time the war hit, streamlining efforts appeared to be paying off. That and unprecedented wartime travel aboard Central trains, however, rendered a false signal to NYC (and other U.S. roads) that people would remain loyal to railroads and ride new trains after the war. Intending to get a lead on this postwar optimism, NYC in 1944 mounted its biggest campaign ever on train modernization by ordering 300 new cars of varying types, principally coaches, diners, lounge cars, and observation-parlor cars. Then, soon after the close of the war in 1945, Central placed an astounding order for yet 420 more new cars—the largest single passenger-car order of any U.S. railroad ever.

Due to the onslaught of car orders from railroads across the land as well as material shortages, deliveries stretched into 1950. By this time, Central had come to the realization that Americans' loyalty to the rail travel had shifted unexpectedly. The postwar era had brought new manufacturing power to America and new buying power to its people—and they wanted to buy automobiles to ride on new highways being funded by federal and local governments.

Regardless, NYC had plunged ahead as the huge, 720-car order trickled in from Pullman-Standard, the Budd Company, and American Car & Foundry. In 1948, the *James Whitcomb Riley* had been totally re-equipped with new

cars. In 1949, the *Century* was also re-equipped, and its 1938 cars bumped to the *Commodore* and other trains. The *Pacemaker* also received all-new cars that year while the *Chicago Mercury, New England States, Southwestern Limited, Ohio State Limited, Detroiter,* and *Twilight Limited* (Chicago–Detroit) received enough new cars, together with their pre-war lightweights, to now feature all-streamlined equipment. Many of these trains were now dieselized.

Central went all out advertising its new "Dreamliners," placing a memorable series of ads in national magazines. New cars and trains were introduced amid great fanfare and publicity. But it was largely to no avail. By 1951, patronage was off by 32 percent from three years prior, and NYC had to address how it could reduce costs. One solution had been to replace expensive-to-operate locomotive-hauled local trains of low patronage on branch and secondary lines with new, self-propelled Budd-built Rail Diesel Cars—RDCs. Another solution was to combine duplicative services, and so the all-Pullman *Advance Commodore Vanderbilt* was combined with the all-coach

A husky Niagara wheels an advance section of the New York–Chicago *North Shore Limited* along the Hudson near Oscawana, New York, in 1946. The presence of open-window "local" coaches suggests that the extra section of train 39 is being run to accommodate an overflow of passengers destined for Poughkeepsie and Albany. The *North Shore Limited* operated to Chicago via the Canadian Southern along the north shore of Lake Erie to Detroit, hence the name. *J. R. Quinn, Big Four Graphics/Jay Williams collection*

Sporting two stainless-steel Santa Fe sleepers that will operate through to the West Coast, the westbound *20th Century Limited* pauses at Englewood Station on Chicago's South Side on August 11, 1956. The through sleepers will be handed over to Santa Fe's *Super Chief*. Departing Englewood, the handsome two-tone gray *Century* shows off its sleeper-bar-lounge observation car, the *Sandy Creek*, built in 1949. *Both photos, John Dziobko*

Pacemaker into a single train since the two ran on similar schedules, though both trains continued to be marketed separately. This cut operating-crew (engineer, fireman, brakemen) costs—labor being one of the highest costs in railroading. By 1953, Central was losing nearly $53 million annually on passenger service.

In 1954, the bold Robert R. Young gained control of the NYC which by this time was nearly bankrupt. A pro-passenger man, Young vowed to solve the passenger situation—in a positive way—through a number of tactics, his pet one being "Train-X." A "super lightweight" streamliner of radical (read, unproven) technology—a Baldwin hydraulic-transmission diesel locomotive hauling low-slung "Talgo"-type (single-axle) cars—Train-X made its debut as *The Xplorer* in January 1956. Young

had a big party planned for its round-trip Detroit–Chicago publicity run, and the guest list included a plethora of railroad and car-builder officials along with high-society types, including Hollywood stars. Unfortunately, the ride was as rough as a buckboard wagon, even on carefully groomed track.

The Xplorer was joined by a second experimental train in 1956. General Motors' *Aerotrain* was another super lightweight, though of more conventional technology, including a futuristic locomotive that harbored a standard Electro-Motive diesel engine. *The Xplorer* entered service on the Cleveland–Columbus–Dayton–Cincinnati corridor while the GM train—not owned by NYC but operated by GM for promotional purposes—became the *Great Lakes Aerotrain* operating between Chicago and Cleveland (complete with "Cruisin' Susan" meals served seatside). The *Aerotrain* barnstormed on to other railroads and was only moderately more successful than *The Xplorer*, which in fact turned out to be a disaster and was withdrawn from service by 1958.

Also in 1956, as the Interstate Highway Act was passed, the Interstate Commerce Commission investigated the railroad industry's claim that passenger service was now widely being operated at a loss. Critics were counterclaiming that the railroads were guilty of perpetrating a myth, and that the losses were really hype calculated to justify the swell of passenger-service abandonments. During the hearings it was determined that railroads were indeed experiencing heavy losses on intercity passenger operations and that ridership was at all-time low levels. As a result, the Central, among other roads, was permitted to gradually begin trimming the biggest revenue losers from its timetables. That year, Central reduced its annual scheduled passenger train-miles by 3.6 million (about 9,500 train-miles a day or the equivalent of about ten Chicago–New York trips), and in 1957 another 4.5 million train-miles were cut.

Young was reluctant to eliminate service, but in 1958 he eliminated himself, and Alfred Perlman quickly stepped in to speed the necessary reductions along. The *Commodore Vanderbilt*—by this time a coach and Pullman train—and the *Century* were combined. Else-where, other services likewise were consolidated, such as the *Southwestern* and the *Ohio State Limited* between New York and Cleveland, where they split and went their separate ways. The railroad terminated its contract with the Pullman Company and began operating its own sleeping cars. NYC had even gone so far as to sell many of its passenger depots to private concerns.

The strategies worked. Losses were cut from $38 million in 1955 to $16 million in the mid 1960s. In the face of the decimation, there were bright spots. In 1959 NYC experimented with new economy sleepers—"Sleepercoaches" (Budd-built Slumbercoaches)—and wound up jointly building a small fleet of its own budget sleepers with Budd. In 1960 certain amenities were restored to the *20th Century Limited* and in 1962 *Century* equipment was refurbished for the train's 60th anniversary.

Unfortunately, although losses had been significantly curtailed, those that had caused them—customer preference for other transportation modes, escalating labor costs, subsidized competition—did not go away. The Central was resigned to the fact that there was a limited future for the passenger train, and cuts continued throughout the system. Some passenger trains had shrunk to single-car operations. The once-mighty *Mercury*, for example, was at times operated with a single RDC. In 1966, the Central made one last (and very curious) defense for the future of passenger-train

From the sublime to the ridiculous. . . at the opposite extreme to the *Century* were little trains such as this at Niagara Falls, New York, serving as a connection to and from mainline trains at Buffalo. *John Dziobko*

service by outfitting an RDC with roof-mounted jet engines and an aerodyamically swooping nose. NYC operated the bizarre contraption at close to 184 miles per hour over a stretch of Water Level Route main line in northern Indiana. Central's belief at the time was that the future of U.S. passenger railroading lay in high-speed, short-haul corridors and that this special experiment was linked to that.

Hindsight now indicates that Central may not have been far off the mark as high-speed corridor service in the U.S. gains new momentum at the close of the century. Regardless, NYC quietly dismantled the test car, having set the stage for the railroad's final chapter in passenger railroading. In late 1967, the Central abruptly announced the termination of the *20th Century Limited*, and on December 2 of that year, the trains made their final departures from New York and Chicago. The following day, a "new" replacement train—nameless Nos. 27 and 28 with a basic consist of coaches, diner-lounge, and sleepers—began running between Chicago and New York/Boston as Central began a movement to replace long-distance services with a series of short-haul connecting corridor runs: e.g., Chicago–Cleveland, New York–Buffalo, Chicago–Detroit.

It was all pretty much moot. On February 1, 1968, New York Central vanished into the Penn Central merger. The move to all-corridor services was suspended, although cuts continued until Congress rendered a stay of execution for the American passenger train until a nationwide solution could be developed. Such was the infant beginning of Amtrak, which would come on line in 1971.

CENTRAL SUBURBAN SERVICES

NYC operated suburban-type passenger service in Chicago, Pittsburgh (through P&LE), Boston, and metropolitan New York. Services at Chicago were modest at best, consisting in later years of but a single Elkhart–Chicago local, discontinued early in the 1960s. The P&LE service west from Pittsburgh once went all the way to Youngstown, Ohio, but later was cut back to College, Pennsylvania. P&LE services lasted into the 1980s. The Boston & Albany commuter service ran between Boston, Riverside (two routes between Boston and Riverside), Framingham, and Worcester, 44 miles, along with two branches, and much is still in operation under the Massachusetts Bay Transportation Authority. All of these suburban operations were steam and later diesel-

Self-propelled electric multiple-unit (M.U.) cars were the staple of NYC suburban services in metropolitan New York. This three-car M.U. set has just departed the Spuyten Duyvil station in the spring of 1964 and is about to swing in agains the Hudson River. In the background is the West Side Freight Line, nee Hudson River Railroad's main line to Chambers Street in Manhattan. *Richard J. Solomon*

operated and in the big NYC picture were relatively modest endeavors.

Such was not the case for New York City, where Central held a commanding and strategic presence in the realm of suburban services. Of first importance was the Harlem Line commuter services between Grand Central and Pawling, 64 miles. The majority of NYC service on the Harlem was between Grand Central and the end of electrification at White Plains/North White Plains, 23 miles out. Most service in this sector was provided by M.U. cars—the mainstay of NYC commuter service—and some electric locomotive-hauled trains. Suburban train service beyond to Brewster, 54 miles, and Pawling was provided by locomotive-hauled trains which changed from electric locomotives to steam (later diesel) power at White Plains North Station. In some cases, cross-platforms connections were provided between M.U. trains and locomotive-hauled trains at North White Plains. Local intercity service all the way to Chatham was provided until 1971 when it was discontinued under the new Amtrak law.

Of second importance important was the Hudson Line to Poughkeepsie, 73 miles out of Grand Central. Most Hudson Line service was concentrated on the electrified portion of this route, between Grand Central and Croton-Harmon, 33 miles, and like the Harlem operated largely with M.U. cars but also electric locomotive-hauled trains. Service beyond to Peekskill and Poughkeepsie was provided by connecting local steam (later, diesel) trains although some trains operated through from Grand Central to Poughkeepsie, changing from electric to steam or diesel locomotives at Harmon as did the long-distance trains.

Between the two above-mentioned commuter routes was the storied Putnam Division commuter district, operating between Sedgwick Avenue (High Bridge) on the Hudson Line and Brewster via Yorktown Heights. "Put" trains were steam- and diesel-powered, and passengers out of Grand Central had to use Hudson Line commuter trains as far as High Bridge where a change of trains was required. Most Put trains terminated at Yorktown Heights, 41 bucolic miles out of Grand Central, but a few wandered beyond as far as Brewster, where they entered the Harlem Line. The Put was a quaint but very money-losing operation whose proximity to the Harlem and Hudson

lines made it vulnerable to abandonment, which happened in the late 1950s.

Another NYC suburban service casualty of that period was that of the West Shore Line. Suburban trains originated at Weehawken, New Jersey, on the Hudson River which required Manhattan passengers to use trans-Hudson ferries out of Cortlandt Street in Manhattan. Most of the steam- (later, diesel) powered trains ran to Haverstraw, New York, 33 miles out of Weehawken, with other suburban runs going as far as Newburgh, New York (57 miles) and a few to Kingston, New York (89 miles) and even Albany, although those can hardly be considered commuter runs. Its growth and popularity hampered by the ferry connection, the West Shore service was another particularly bad financial drain on the Central and it was gone by the 1960s.

Harlem and Hudson Line services were also money-losing propositions during Central's later years, but not to the extent that intercity services were. Patronage was not the problem on these lines as much as the costs of doing business; further, discontinuance of these two services would have been a political nightmare for the railroad. Wisely, NYC and successor Penn Central patiently waited for the State of New York to implement an agency to operate suburban services. Such a movement began in the mid-1960s thanks to New York Governor Nelson A. Rockefeller, and today NYC suburban service is alive and mostly well, operating under local transportation authorities.

An Alco road-switcher scoots along with an unidentified local train on the West Shore at Haworth, New Jersey, on July 18, 1956. The presence of a Railway Post Office and baggage car may indicate this to be an Albany train. *Sherman Dance*

As a descendant of the New York Central, Conrail had operated the majority of former NYC trackage. On August 16, 1997, a Conrail freight lead by a new Electro-Motive SD80MAC diesel cruises along the old Boston & Albany main line through Chester, Massachusetts, and past a restored B&A caboose. *Brian Solomon*

THE NEW YORK CENTRAL TODAY

Though Thrice Removed, NYC Still Holds a Presence

Corporately, the New York Central ceased to exist as of February 1, 1968. But the spirit of the NYC—as beleaguered as it was at that point—clung to life beyond that fateful date. Aside from a few token pieces of equipment that had been painted in Penn Central markings to mark the start of the new era, much remained the same well into the merger.

In fact, that was part of the problem. From the top down both component companies refused to integrate, managing the railroad poorly at best while internally maintaining the "Green Team [NYC] vs. Red Team [PRR]" philosophies that for years had mirrored the railroads' pre-merger rivalry. Stories of bad service getting worse became rampant among shippers as well as passengers. PC's Al Perlman and Stuart Saunders got into it for the final time in 1969 when Perlman requested $25 million to refurbish the PC's freight-car fleet and Saunders refused. Perlman threatened to resign as a final act of defiance, and Saunders insisted on it! By 1970 the PC was losing $100 million dollars annually. The stock market plunged that year as the country reeled from an inflationary recession, and the federal government—worried that PC's failure might trigger a 1929-style crash—guaranteed loans for the corporation. But it was too late. Penn Central declared bankruptcy on June 1, 1970, at that time the largest corporate failure in history, and other Northeastern carriers were swept into the fray.

Congress intervened in two ways. First, a bill was signed into law which created the National Railroad Passenger Corporation—Amtrak—which took over the bulk of U.S. intercity passenger services (a large portion of which was PC's) on May 1, 1971. Then Congress went on to create the United States Railway Association to address the mass railroad bankruptcies of the Northeast. USRA in turn created the Consolidated Rail Corporation—Conrail—to take over six bankrupt carriers (PC, Erie Lackawanna, Jersey Central, Reading, Lehigh Valley, and Lehigh & Hudson River) on April 1, 1976, and begin anew. Route rationalization was high on Conrail's agenda, and numerous unprofitable lines were abandoned or sold off. The best of the former NYC's routes were combined with those of the old PRR, creating new, efficient transportation arteries; passenger-related services were passed on to new operating agencies. Freight service and operations were drastically redefined. Meanwhile, a major, intense program of physical rehabilitation was under way to track, locomotives, rolling stock, and other infrastructure. The result? Conrail became a vital, profitable transportation company that eventually was returned to the private-sector.

As such, Conrail became an extremely attractive piece of property to other railroads, and as the 1990s wound down, a great drama unfolded as Norfolk Southern Corporation vied with CSX Corporation for acquisition of Conrail. Both won the battle, with the Surface Transportation Board ruling that Conrail be split between the two. As this book first went to press, that massive project was under way—one that would make the New York Central thrice removed.

The years since the demise of the NYC have borne many efforts to preserve the heritage of the railroad. One of the more prominent and successful endeavors of late is the new Adirondack Scenic Railroad, which operates along the scenic Adirondack branch north from Utica toward Lake Placid, New York. In this 1998 scene near Forestport, restored NYC Alco road-switcher 8223 (the first RS3 acquired by the NYC) hauls National Railway Historical Society conventioneers on a Utica–Thendara excursion. *Mike Schafer*

Though the Central has been gone for more than 30 years, vestiges remain throughout NYC territory. Witness the old Peoria & Eastern (a Big Four subsidiary) freight-house alongside south-bound U.S. Highway 51 at Bloomington, Illinois, in 1990. *Steve Smedley*

CENTRAL'S LEGACY

No railroad with the presence of the once-mighty New York Central ever goes completely away. Although there is precious little left that bears NYC markings, the railroad left an indelible legacy. Foremost was its world-class New York–Chicago Water Level Route main line. Today, nearly every mile of the 960-mile route remains a vital transportation artery, even as it gets split up between NS and CSX. Between Porter, Indiana, near Chicago, and Schenectady, the line is particularly dense with traffic, largely freight but also passenger. From the Albany/Schenectady area south to New York City the line serves primarily as a high-speed passenger corridor that hosts 100 miles per hour intercity passenger services of Amtrak intertwined with Metro-North commuter trains south of Poughkeepsie. Interestingly, the passenger flagship of today's Water Level Route is Amtrak's *Lake Shore Limited*, which provides services and scheduling remarkably similar to NYC's version of yore. The bulk of freight traffic into metropolitan New York now heads down the old West Shore main line between Schenectady and New Jersey via Selkirk Yard—still a key freight facility. Likewise, traffic on the Boston & Albany between Selkirk Yard and Boston is heavy with freight while the Boston section of the *Lake Shore Limited* serves as the line's principal passenger train. Suburban trains of the MBTA (Massachusetts Bay

Transportation Authority) do the duties established long ago by B&A suburban trains. Basically, CSX will operate the bulk of former NYC lines east of Cleveland to New York, Boston, and Montreal. NS will operate the main line west of Cleveland to Chicago.

The news has not been as bright for the old Michigan Central lines. Little remains of MC's multitude of branches in its home state. As well, the MC as a through route between Buffalo and Chicago has been severed in Canada. Interestingly, though, the Detroit–Porter (Indiana) segment of the main line to Chicago is intact, serving mainly a passenger route for Amtrak—which owns a portion of it—and is the focus of future high-speed services.

Big Four routes have survived fairly well overall. Though long devoid of passenger service, the Cleveland–Galion–Columbus–Cincinnati and Galion–Indianapolis–Terre Haute routes still play an important role in freight traffic, but west of Terre Haute to St. Louis the former-NYC main line is largely history. Meanwhile, the old Toledo & Ohio Central still reaches into the coal fields of West Virginia, and Big Four's old Egyptian Line south from Indiana Harbor still carries some freight, including traffic that bypasses Chicago by traveling south to Schneider, Indiana, thence west on the old Kankakee Belt to the Burlington Northern & Santa Fe at Streator, Illinois. Most of the line south of Schneider to Cairo is gone. The once-high-speed Cincinnati–Indianapolis–Kankakee–Chicago route shares a similar fate, with minimal service and outright abandonment in some segments. Likewise, Big Four's old Peoria & Eastern route is largely out of service, although that between Indianapolis and Crawfordsville, Indiana, now serves as a passenger route for Amtrak.

Although Conrail had been the operator of

most ex-NYC track before the Conrail split-up, "Big Blue" rationalized a large amount of its system by spinning off redundant or unwanted trackage to other carriers, if it wasn't wholly abandoned. The result has been a number of colorful shortline operations, some of which have revived New York Central imagery. For example, the Finger Lakes Railway operates portions of the old Auburn Road (Auburn & Syracuse and Auburn & Rochester) with locomotives painted in Central's black-and-gray freight scheme. Meanwhile, in the Adirondack Mountains, the Adirondack Scenic Railway hauls tourists on passenger cars painted in the 1938 *20th Century Limited* livery pulled by diesels decked out in NYC markings. With help from New York State, the railroad has reopened much of the former Adirondack branch with a goal of restoring the line all the way to Lake Placid, New York.

Elsewhere, museums have sought to preserve New York Central equipment. Famed NYC&HRRR 4-4-0 No. 999 resides at Chicago's Museum of Science and Industry, while passengers riding Amtrak's *Lake Shore Limit-*ed, *Capitol Limited,* and *Pennsylvanian* can glimpse ex-NYC Mohawk 3001 (and some NYC passenger cars) at the National New York Central Railroad Museum at Elkhart, Indiana, near the Amtrak station. Groups such as the Central New York Chapter of the National Railway Historical Society have also preserved NYC's heritage. CNY Chapter has painted two retired Electro-Motive E-series passenger locomotives into the celebrated lightning stripe scheme for use on special excursion trains.

Perhaps the ultimate remaining tribute to the New York Central is Grand Central Terminal. Cherished by New Yorkers as one of the city's most famous landmarks, GCT has been restored to near original appearance and still serves in the capacity for which it originally was intended: as a passenger terminal. Though the sounds of boarding calls for train No. 25, the *20th Century Limited,* are no longer heard, it would not take much effort to imagine what the anticipation would have been like of boarding the world's finest train in the world's finest train station.

In a scene reminiscent of the *20th Century Limited's* evening race along the Hudson (pages 116-117), a Metro-North suburban train skims the banks of the mighty river on a crisp June evening in 1997. Metro-North Railroad operates the former NYC Hudson and Harlem lines services. *Brian Solomon*

INDEX